OWN
ANY
OCCASION

Mastering the Art of
Speaking and Presenting

Erik Palmer

atd
PRESS

T0273679

ATD Press is an internationally renowned source of insightful and practical information on talent development, training, and professional development.

ATD Press
1640 King Street
Alexandria, VA 22314 USA

Ordering information: Books published by ATD Press can be purchased by visiting ATD's website at www.td.org/books or by calling 800.628.2783 or 703.683.8100.

Library of Congress Control Number: 2017948359

ISBN-10: 1-56286-685-0
ISBN-13: 978-1-56286-685-3
e-ISBN: 978-1-56286-771-3

ATD Press Editorial Staff
Director: Kristine Luecker
Manager: Melissa Jones
Community of Practice Manager, Career Development: Sue Kaiden
Developmental Editor: Christian Green
Text Design: Iris Sanchez
Cover Design: Faceout Studio, Derek Thorton

Printed by Versa Press Inc, East Peoria, IL

Contents

*For Greg and Ross, who became excellent speakers and fine men.
I'm proud of you.*

And for Anne, who listened and encouraged.

Introduction

Speaking matters.

You know that. And you recognize the great benefits that come with being well spoken. But you also know that oral communication skills can always be improved. Even brilliant, successful people, some with careers that involve daily high-level oral communication, still seek help. They don't feel confident or competent in all speaking situations. Let me share some personal examples of people who were motivated to seek my help.

Michael was the chief justice of the Supreme Court of a western state. Every year, when the new session of the legislature convenes, the assembled houses hear the "State of the State" from the governor and a "State of the Judiciary" from the chief justice. Michael wanted help crafting and delivering his speech. He believed the ones he'd given in the past were not as impressive as they could have been.

Dan works for one of the world's largest mining companies. He is a master electrician, and had trained electricians for a local company for years before being hired by his current employer. He was such a good electrician that his new employer tasked him with developing and delivering training materials for company electricians around the globe. He wasn't confident about his communication skills.

Katie was asked to facilitate a meeting of nurses to develop a better pressure-ulcer prevention program at the health facility they worked for. She was not satisfied with the training materials, but didn't have a clear idea of what could be improved.

Scott worked for a firm that helps retail clients find locations in shopping centers. While he was fine handling paperwork, he wanted to be part of the discussions with clients, where the big money was made.

Karla worked for a large CPA firm. Because of a new promotion, she began leading weekly meetings for her staff, but she didn't feel comfortable leading meetings.

Kelly was tasked with creating webinars for an association of nursing-home therapists. Now, therapists everywhere would be able to see and hear her, rather than just read the articles she had been writing for the association's journal.

Tom, a family practice doctor, was chosen to head all the family practice doctors affiliated with a major hospital. The new position required speaking in front of many doctors. Debbie wanted to make effective videos to promote her network marketing company. Betsy was a psychotherapist who wanted to get more business by speaking to clubs and organizations. Patrick needed to give speeches to raise money for the nonprofit TV station he worked for.

It's not just workplace worries that create a desire to improve oral communication skills, however. Sam wanted to be more effective coaching Pee Wee football and leading Bible study at his church. Eva was worried about the toast she was going to give at her daughter's wedding. Tanya wanted to speak better because conversations with her in-laws intimidated her. Mary Beth won her state's Miss Rodeo contest, but she and 11 other contestants in the Miss Rodeo America pageant wanted help with the pageant's oral performance piece.

Do you identify with any of these people? Most of us are called upon to use speaking skills every day. Are you confident in your oral communication skills? Do you believe they are adequate for the demands of your workplace or life? How many significant events will occur in your life in which your ability to speak well will matter?

Few People Speak Well

Although speaking is important, you have probably noticed that few people speak well. Start with the workplace. Maybe you have been bored at a staff meeting. Perhaps you've had difficulty understanding what a co-worker was attempting to explain. Maybe you have suffered through a dreadful webinar. Perhaps a professional facilitator in a training environment left you flat. Maybe you have been stunned by the poor verbal communication skills of a person you were interviewing for a job.

Now think about your social situations. Maybe you watched an awkward after-dinner speech or toast. Perhaps you talked to someone and noticed how inarticulate he was. Maybe the president of your service club or the principal at your child's school didn't speak as well as you expected. No doubt you can think of someone who impressed you, but I am certain that you have many more examples of people who were quite unimpressive.

You may even know people who often speak in front of groups, but still haven't mastered the art of speaking well. For example, I attended an awards dinner for many years that was designed to honor excellent employees at my business. Everett organized the annual event and always chose himself to be the emcee—year after year after year. He certainly relished his moment in the spotlight, but he was dreadfully boring—monotonous, humorless, rambling, and dull. Everett somehow managed to take the joy out of the event. Years of hosting it did not make him any better. This is why becoming an effective oral communicator will put you ahead of even experienced speakers.

Be More Successful

People who speak well are more successful than people who don't speak well. Not only does this apply to professions in which speaking plays an integral role, such as a trial attorney, motivational speaker, facilitator, professor, or trainer; it also applies to every other profession. No landscaper can get a contract without being able to communicate clearly. A hairdresser who is fun to talk to will have more business. Think of your workplace. Wouldn't everyone benefit from improved oral communication? Of course! Mastering verbal communication skills dramatically increases *your* chance of business success as well. Research shows that employers rank verbal communication as the number one competency they value in employees.

The National Association of Colleges and Employers (NACE) surveys employers every year to see what skills they value. In NACE's "Job Outlook

2016," the skill that had the highest weighted average value was the "ability to verbally communicate with persons inside and outside the organization" (Williams 2016). The University of Kent combined results from a number of surveys from Microsoft, Target Jobs, the BBC, Prospects, NACE, AGR, and other organizations to determine which skills were most often deemed important. At the top of the list? Verbal communication.

And there is a good reason—verbal skills have been shown to contribute to workplace success. A study by two Stanford professors followed MBA graduates for 20 years after graduation and found that a good portion of an executive's environment is verbal. Further, chief executives spend 70 to 80 percent of their time speaking or listening, and the majority of top achievers rated their oral skills at the "top of the scale." The study's conclusion was that "talking and persuading indeed are essential to the manager's success" (Harrell and Alpert 1986).

But as I mentioned, speaking well is not just a business skill. You'll also find that enhancing these skills will help you be more effective when communicating with your partner, your children, or the other people you interact with on a given day. You will be better able to advocate for your child at the parent-teacher conference. You will be more successful getting the refund for a defective product or substandard service. You'll have the confidence to speak at the retirement dinner, the bachelorette party, the awards ceremony, or simply in everyday social situations.

Why This Book?

I am not the first to recognize the importance of speaking well and to notice that few have mastered the art. Many people feel the pressure to improve their oral communication skills, and many people and businesses have responded to that desire. Just look in the business section of your local bookstore or an online retailer—you'll find multiple books that have something to do with speaking. Some focus on general presentation skills, some on preparing speeches for specific events, and others on specific skills such as closing the deal, negotiating, overcoming fear, speaking in social settings, or creating PowerPoint presentations. They all have useful tips if you have time to sort through all their pages.

But what if you don't want a 210-page book about negotiating a real estate deal, a 189-page book about communicating with negative employees, or a 245-page book about making a better PowerPoint presentation? What if you won't be on stage at TED or do presentations like Steve Jobs? What if you just want a book that simplifies the process of effective communication, rather than complicating it with advice about random speaking techniques?

This book is for people who want to speak better in general. It outlines how to be an effective speaker in all situations. The steps you need to take to be impressive in a job interview are the same steps that will help you succeed in front of an auditorium full of people. Preparing for an after-dinner speech involves the same process as preparing for a sales call. Getting ready to meet the in-laws requires the same thinking as getting ready to train new employees.

This book starts with a different perspective—that of teacher and trainer. I have spent decades in classrooms and offices teaching oral communication skills. Teaching is all about taking complex things and breaking them into simpler, teachable parts. It is also about teaching skills in order. You weren't taught about paragraphs until you were first taught about sentences; you weren't taught about sentences until you were taught about words; you weren't taught about words until you learned about letters. I think you will find the teacher's perspective easy to follow and easy to remember. If your English teacher did a good job teaching you how to write, you can write a paragraph on any topic. If I teach you well in this book, you will be able to speak well in any situation.

The path to becoming comfortable and competent as a speaker is easier to follow than all the books on the topic would lead you to believe. This is not to say that becoming an effective oral communicator is easy. It's like building a house. Without an effective blueprint, you have no chance to succeed. But once you have the blueprint, there is some serious work involved before the house is complete. This book is the blueprint for speaking. The steps to follow are simple, but there is effort involved in becoming an impressive speaker.

I may share some ideas that were in the back of your mind, but never given much thought. There will be some ideas that cause you to totally rethink speaking. If you already have a lot of speaking experience, you may have moments of "I already knew that," but you'll also gain new insights. Some elements of effective oral communication will be easy for you to master, while others will be more difficult. What is difficult for you may be easy for someone else, and what you find easy will challenge others. We may all start at different places, but by the end of the book you will have the understanding and tools you need to be an effective speaker.

It Isn't Just About "Public Speaking"

Most people think of public speaking as capital-*P*, capital-*S* "Public Speaking"—some type of occasion in which we need to use formal language while standing in front of a large group. However, when I refer to speaking throughout the book, I am not referring to only a formal presentation in front of a large audience, but all the forms of speaking beyond casual banter with friends. Speaking encompasses a wide variety of genres: interviews, training sessions, arguments, toasts, stage presentations, answering questions in a meeting, facilitating negotiations, working with clients, making sales calls, delivering webinars, creating podcasts, and many more. The framework I share for effective oral communication is involved in all those situations.

Don't worry. You don't need to become a master orator. You don't need to compete with the motivational speaker your firm hired for the company retreat or the televangelist who can make his congregation laugh, cry, and shout during a 30-minute sermon. Don't feel intimidated by that kind of talent. You simply have to understand how those orators create their magic and apply that understanding to improve your own communication skills. Your goal is to become more confident, more competent, and more impressive as a speaker—in short, to own any occasion.

Part 1

Before You Speak

At the Academy Awards, there are Oscars for screenwriting and there are Oscars for acting. In other words, some people are awarded for coming up with the right words, while others are awarded for saying them. This reveals an important but always overlooked insight into the art of oral communication. All speaking involves two distinct parts: creating a talk and performing a talk. *Creating* refers to everything done before you open your mouth; *performing* refers to everything you do as you are speaking.

Few of us have writers to create a script for us or can hire performers to speak for us. This means that we must master both parts ourselves because all effective oral communication demands both. You may be confident that you have a screenwriter's talents—you can come up with something worth saying, but are not necessarily confident saying it. Or you may believe you are a talented performer—comfortable speaking but concerned about the value of what you have to say. Or, you may think you are adept at both creating and performing, even though your audiences would strongly disagree. No matter where you are as a speaker, you can and will improve at both creating and performing your talks using the ideas in this book.

In part 1, the focus is on creating a talk—what you should do before you open your mouth. Obviously, speakers must create the message before they can say it. Sometimes that message is created for us. In the workplace, corporate trainers are hired to present certain information, and managers may have to address certain topics. Sometimes we create our own messages. Often this happens very quickly, without even realizing we just invented something to say. For example, if I think the umpire made a bad call on strike three, my words come out immediately. At other times, we may work hard trying to come up with something to say, as I did before I dropped my son off at college a few years ago. But no matter the situation, we should be aware that we create the message before we speak it, whether the message is for one person or many, for in-person or digital talks, for work or for pleasure.

Rule 1: Never speak unless you have something worth saying.

You can think of people who violate that rule, but you do not want to be one of them. You want to craft an excellent talk, build a memorable speech, and impress every listener. Creating effective messages requires more than words, just as movies involve lighting, sets, and costumes in addition to screenwriting before the actors show up. In this section, I'll share the five steps that guarantee a well-built talk.

Step 1: Audience

Nancy was the superintendent of schools for my local school district. Superintendents are asked to speak at Parent-Teacher Community Organization (PTCO) meetings, and I saw her often at PTCO meetings at our school. From the moment Nancy entered the room, she was personally engaging with people: "Hi, Jim. How's your son doing? I heard that he got injured in the game last week." "Karen! Enjoying the move from ninth grade to 11th grade?"

As she spoke, it was clear that she knew specific details about our school, not just general details about the entire district. It felt like we were listening to a friend and neighbor. Nancy knew about her audience.

Each Speech Is Different

Do you speak the same way in the boardroom as you do in the break room? If you do, you might not have your job for long. Should you use the same words with a prospective employer that you use with your teammates in the dugout? Probably not, if you want to be hired. If you were asked to give a five-minute speech on office behavior, shouldn't your first question be, "For whom?" It makes a difference if that speech is going to be for new employees, the CEO, your co-workers, or a comedy club audience. Adjust your speech to suit the situation.

Many speakers miss this point. When I train people, the message I share is essentially the same everywhere I go, yet my workshops in Saudi Arabia are quite different from my workshops in California. I make significant changes to my instructional design. While this may be an extreme example, it highlights this essential concept, which applies in non-work-related talks as well. (I will bounce back and forth between workplace examples and nonworkplace examples throughout this book to emphasize the broad applicability of the communication concepts.) You build a very different speech for graduates of the Electrical Apprenticeship and Training Committee than you do for graduates of Greendale High School, even though both are graduation speeches. The EATC graduates are generally older, have job experience, and are headed straight to a career as electricians. High school graduates are younger, largely inexperienced, and headed off to college, entry level jobs, or places such as the electrical apprenticeship school. Your best wishes for the future should be specific to the very different immediate futures that each audience has. Impressive speakers never use a generic speech because they know that to be truly successful, they must tailor the talk to fit their audience. You, too, should never consider making a presentation of any sort without analyzing the audience, whether that audience is one person, several people, or a crowd; in the workplace or in social situations; in-person or online. Modify your words for maximum impact with every listener. Most speakers don't spend enough time understanding the intended audience. Too many times, speakers simply go through their agenda—often created without the listeners in mind.

Consider Your Audience

Recall that I spent some time teaching. I once attended a staff meeting that was scheduled for 4 p.m. on Friday, where a facilitator came in to work us through the process of developing some new procedures for dealing with problem students. She put up PowerPoint slide after PowerPoint slide, each filled with densely packed text or slick graphics with arrows indicating the feedback loops and processes. Perhaps this presentation worked elsewhere—she had already given it to staff at other schools in our district—but we hated it. Why? The facilitator did not understand the mindset of the audience at 4 p.m. on a Friday. I have attended staff meetings where the facilitator spent 20 minutes going over information that everyone already knew, as well as meetings where the facilitator assumed the audience was familiar with a situation when in fact no one had any idea what he was talking about.

I once watched a local television celebrity give a canned speech at my children's school, asking students to "stay in school and stay away from gangs." At a wealthy, suburban school with a 98 percent graduation rate? A great message—just not for this audience. I am sure you have your own examples of occasions when a speaker misjudged the audience. Avoid these mistakes. Analyze the audience.

That's Why Focus Groups Exist

Some businesses take dramatic steps to understand their audience. You have heard of companies that pull together focus groups, right? The real purpose of the focus group is to understand the audience. Before a product is released, an audience composed of members of the target market is assembled. The company will try to learn everything it can about the group—its biases, its interests, and its desires—to design an effective product launch. One example of this is Red Bull, which grew from a small product in Thailand to one of the most popular brands in the world in just 20 years. The company succeeded by totally understanding its audience. It sponsors events its target market loves (windsurfing, motocross, snowboarding, and other extreme sports), and it puts its logo on clothing styles that are popular with the targeted demographic. The company's knowledge of its audience has translated into huge success.

Other types of businesses also understand the value of analyzing their audience. Years ago, I got a phone call inviting me to spend a day at a law firm to be on a mock jury. It seems there are firms that specialize in jury selection. Before a major trial, firms hire experts to analyze potential jurors and assist in voir dire, the process of selecting the people who will sit on the jury for a trial. The analysts get quite specific: Argument A was very persuasive to females without college degrees age 18 to 35, but did not persuade college-educated women age 18 to 35; argument B was very persuasive to males age 25 to 40, but was not persuasive to males over 40; in general, men agreed with the plaintiff in the case, whereas women tended to find for the defendant. With this information, when the case gets to court, the lawyers can try to select jury members who are most sympathetic to the firm's arguments or adjust their arguments if the jury makeup is not what the firm wanted. If companies are spending millions of dollars analyzing audiences, don't you think you should spend more time analyzing your listeners?

Find Out as Much as You Can

Find out everything you can about your listeners before you write your talk. It isn't hard to think of situations in which this information is crucial. Before an interview, isn't it important to find out who will be interviewing you? Should you emphasize your writing skills or your collaboration skills? You need to know something about the business you are applying for and what that business is looking for in prospective employees.

Before a sales presentation, isn't it important to ask a few questions about your potential customer? What does the buyer already know about the product? What is the most important feature in her mind? Is she going to want a logical presentation with facts only or should the focus be on gaining friendship and trust? What does your competitor offer?

Before presenting at the staff meeting, shouldn't you find out if everyone agrees or if your ideas are likely to be met with hostility, whether open or subtle?

Key Questions to Consider

For every communication situation, asking questions will enable you to custom-fit your talk. Here are typical questions you can ask before creating your message. Not all will apply to every situation—some are clearly designed for large audiences, some for workplace talks, some for casual talks. While modifications may be needed, these are a good place to start.

How Large Is Your Audience?

One reason to care about the size of the audience is to avoid the surprise factor. Somehow a crowd of 400 is often more intimidating than a group of 40, and you need to mentally prepare for the size of the group. (To some, a group of five is also more intimidating than a group of 40—they believe the closeness will make it easier to notice their mistakes.) Smaller groups may also require a more casual form of speech.

Additionally, you need to think about the logistical adjustments. How many handouts should you bring? What type of activities can you do? Think about your volume level; do you need to use a microphone? Do you need to resize any visual aids?

Where Will the Audience Be?

If you are planning an interactive training course, you need to know that the room will be set up for that. Will listeners be seated at tables or in rows? You can use different activities with groups of eight people around a table than you can with people seated theater-style. Are you going to be facing the audience or performing in the round? You'll want to practice differently if the toast comes from the dance floor in the middle of the room rather than from a podium. If the audience will be standing at the time (as is often the case for quick meetings), shorten your remarks.

How Tired Is the Audience?

A two-hour training session at 3 p.m. cannot be the same as a training session at 9 a.m. Hour two cannot have the same format as hour one. Ears get worn out, and people get tired of sitting. If I present later in the day and have been given 20 to 30 minutes to speak, I move to the shorter end of the range and remove some pieces from the agenda. One study suggests that after 15 minutes, less than half of an audience is paying full attention (Mills 1977). Late in the day, it is probably much less than half. Yes, you think it is a good story, but now is not the time.

Here's another version of tired: I once attended a wedding where the father of the bride gave his toast—his six-page, single-spaced toast—after two hours of an open bar. Had he thought about his audience, he would not have been surprised that most of us stopped listening seven minutes into his 24-minute speech. We were hungry and anxious to get to the buffet. Yet there he stood, repeatedly asking us to quiet down and give him a few more minutes of attention.

What Is Their Average Age and Age Range?

Often a good point is lost because it is not couched in an age-appropriate way. You should not use a *Casablanca* reference with your grandson or a Pokemon Go reference with your grandmother. When I speak to people much younger than I am at training sessions, I adjust my talk—but don't pander. Don't try to get all up in their business to avoid being zero chill. Adding language that doesn't fit your style will work exactly as well as *all up in their business* and *zero chill* worked in the previous sentence. But you do need to know what matches the interests of your audience.

What Is the Audience's Educational Background?

Pick up an issue of *Time* magazine and an issue of *Harper's* magazine. They have very different requirements regarding article length and vocabulary choice. It's clear that they are designed for different audiences. Which one would you prefer to read? Similarly, an audience prefers a speech at their level. You have undoubtedly encountered a trainer who treated you as if you were a schoolkid, and you probably have had an experience with a speaker who was trying to show off her vastly superior knowledge.

It's important to learn key words that the audience knows. A very bright friend of mine had seen the word *placebo* in print but had never heard it pronounced. In a sales pitch to a group of doctors he mentioned the "PLACE-boh" effect, not knowing, as every doctor does, that the word is pronounced "pluh-CEE-boh." It's a small error, but one that cost him a large amount of credibility.

What Does the Audience Know About the Topic?

Do you need to explain the product features to a customer who already has the product and is just deciding whether to buy another? At an engagement party, why would you tell a story about how Kevin and Diane met if all attendees already know how Kevin and Diane met? Figure out how familiar the audience is with the ideas you are going to present. It's not helpful to say, "I know you already know this, but let me just go over it again."

What Does the Audience Want?

Most managers focus on what they want to say. They have a set agenda: Here is the new organizational chart for the firm; here are the new sales targets; this is the new "improve office morale" initiative; this is the way to do this procedure. The trick is that the audience may not want the program being delivered. For example, to effectively explain the new organizational structure, you should figure out what the staff want to know about it. Yes, they want to know who reports to whom, but maybe they also want to know why the change was made, who made the decision, if it is a lasting change, and how they will personally be affected.

When I attended my son's graduation from Pomona College, the commencement speaker was the prominent anchorman Walter Cronkite. At the time, the Iraq war had just begun, and his speech was essentially about the folly of the war and how the lessons of Vietnam had been forgotten. He warned the graduates that the world was in a horrible state and things were bleaker now than they had been in almost any time he could recall. I'm sure many people thought Cronkite was correct, but still, what a downer of a commencement speech! The world is horrible? In a world as bleak as this, who cares about your degree? Commencement speeches are supposed to celebrate accomplishments and send kids off with best wishes and hope for the future. Yes, Cronkite avoided clichés as I recommend later, but his general tone was inappropriate for the occasion. He should have given more thought about what his audience would want in a commencement speech.

Is the Audience Likely to Be Receptive?

Listeners come to your talk with preconceived notions. I once worked for an organization that had a new latest-and-greatest practice every year that the staff needed to be trained on. Anyone who had been with the organization for a length of time got pretty cynical, myself included. If you know the employees are in that position, be more aggressive in persuading them that this program is different from all the others. (If the program isn't different, don't do it!) If you know they are receptive, you don't have to waste time with those explanations. Many employees come into compulsory training sessions with a negative attitude, so be prepared for that. At your neighborhood association meeting, know which neighbors are likely to oppose the fence replacement project. Be ready for them.

What Are Their Biases?

If you walk into the National Rifle Association meeting with an anti-gun pitch, you should not be surprised if you receive a very cool reception. That is an obvious case of bias, and your job as a speaker is to find out the obvious and the not-so-obvious cases. Sometimes, understanding the bias means understanding what topics to avoid. It is also useful to know the political orientation. If an audience has a liberal, conservative, feminist, or other political posture, you need to know that. Don't lie about your beliefs to fool them, but you can keep some of your beliefs to yourself as the situation warrants. Maintain neutrality in the workplace.

What Are Their Interests?

This will be discussed in more detail in chapter 7, but it's important to pick up some things you can use to relate to the audience. Years ago, when I was running a commodity brokerage firm, I went to a breakfast meeting in Goodland, Kansas, to try to convince some farmers to open accounts with my company. My pitch was a disaster. I had my agenda and my standard sales talk about the importance of commodity trading and hedging, but I had no idea what their life was like, and I had no way to connect with them. I didn't even know biscuits and gravy was a breakfast item. I was simply a young city slicker who hadn't taken the time to find out the slightest things about their lives. And it was clear to the audience. You could see "Who is this punk?" written on their faces, and many walked out before I finished.

Make sure you find out nontopical things about your audience to avoid making the huge mistake I made. What does the audience do in their spare time? Do they hunt? Scrapbook? What sports teams do they follow? And food, that's always a good topic. Know about popular restaurants and food choices in the area. (You now know that biscuits and gravy is popular for breakfast in the Midwest!)

Are There Geographical or Regional Factors to Consider?

Do you believe that people in Manhattan, New York, are going to be the same as the people in Manhattan, Kansas? What about an audience in Seattle, Washington, compared with Selma, Alabama? Certainly, there will be more similarities than differences, but there will be differences. For example, after waiting for the roar of laughter to die down, comedian Ron White told a Denver audience that he had told the same joke in Georgia earlier on the tour and got no reaction. It happens.

Don't think only of cultural differences from one region to the next. Are there local festivals happening? Is the area known for a local landmark? When I was in Plymouth, Massachusetts, I made a point of visiting Plymouth Rock before my talk and tossed in a comment about it. Are there other kinds of local features that residents are proud of? And don't go to Milan, Ohio, and say "mih-LAHN." They pronounce it "MY-lun."

Are There Any Cultural Issues?

When I trained educational leaders in Riyadh, Saudi Arabia, the classroom environment was very different from that of other programs I have led. The male teachers were on one side of the room, the female teachers on the other, and a divider was placed between the two groups. The men and women never mixed, even in small group activities, and it would have been totally inappropriate for me to say to one of the women, "Here, these two men need another person for this three-person activity, so you go join them."

Again, that situation is more extreme than most, but cultures do differ. Western cultures tend to be individualistic and motivated by competition; Eastern cultures tend to be group-oriented and value cooperation. And remember, culture does not refer only to racial, religious, or ethnic groups. A football team's culture is different from the marching band's culture, and a speaker at the awards banquet should understand the difference.

What Is Their Mood?

The office mood at 4 p.m. Friday is different from the mood at 8 a.m. Monday or 12 p.m. Wednesday. Occasionally, it may be your job to adjust the mood of the audience. My sister, for example, works for a company that provides outplacement services, and she is called in to work with people who have just been laid off. She has to pick them up off the floor and inspire them to begin their search for a new career. She can't begin by being overly cheerful about their exciting new opportunities; a somber start is needed to match their mood before trying to change the tone.

At some point in your life you will be asked to speak at social events. Obviously, the mood at a eulogy is different from the mood at a bachelor party, and a story that works in one place may be a disaster in the other. Be aware, though, of more nuanced moods every time you speak.

What Motivates Them?

People are motivated by different things. I have a friend who reads *Consumer Reports* and checks many online sites before making any purchase. I have another friend who bought a case of beer he had never heard of before because someone representing the brewery gave away coasters with the brewery's logo at the store that evening. I bet you have a friend who wants to save money on everything, as well as a friend who will overpay simply to have the status of owning the latest, coolest thing, right? The former is driven by logic, whereas the latter is driven by emotion.

I believe that most people are in that second group and offer Apple as proof. Apple has made the emotional connection a huge part of their business model. When a new iPhone is released, customers wait in lines that snake around the block. Are their old phones broken? No. Did all of them study the specifications of the new phone and compare them with other smartphones? Probably not. They just love Apple and love the feeling they get from being among the first to own Apple's latest product.

As a facilitator, manager, or trainer, do not assume that all listeners share your motivation. Indeed, do not assume that all listeners have the same motivation. Offer something that appeals to your specific audience.

It's Worth the Effort

Gathering all that information seems like a lot of work, and it is not always possible to get all the data you want. However, it is well worth the effort; sometimes it's even crucial. My doctor tells a story of a drug representative who wanted to talk to another doctor in the office, but he would never agree to meet. The drug rep offered to bring in lunch for the office to entice the doctor to show up, but even free food was not enough. The doctor didn't show up. During the lunch, though, the sales rep found out that the doctor loved hot dogs and considered himself to be a hot dog connoisseur. So the sales rep offered to do another lunch—with hot dogs—and sure enough, the doctor came. But he didn't stay long because the sales rep only brought ketchup. Any hot dog aficionado knows that hot dogs should be paired with mustard. The sale was lost. Learning everything you can about your listeners enables you to tailor your message to perfectly fit the audience.

Getting the Information

How can you get information? Visit the group or company website. Talk to a member of the organization or to the person who invited you to speak. Query the head of the department about the group. Read a local paper to pick up something about the community. Talk to someone in the same field or who fits the same demographic as the people you will be addressing. Send questions to the organizer. Visit the site of the speech in advance. Be creative to find the information that will allow you to get inside the head of the listener.

Sometimes you don't have the option of gathering information in advance. If a prospective buyer walks onto your sales floor, try to collect all the information you can in your first few minutes of conversation. It shouldn't seem like an interrogation, but you should sneak in questions like the ones discussed in this chapter. Don't let something like ketchup get in the way of your success!

The Devil You Know

A final caveat: Don't forget to apply an audience analysis to groups you know well. For example, the seven people on Marcus's team have all been with him for a while: between 18 months and six years. They know one another well, so this should be the easiest possible audience to analyze. However, these types of groups are often taken for granted. It is easy to fall into a trap such as, "Well that's just how Sam is. She is cynical about everything. Don't worry about it." Do worry about it. If Marcus writes off Sam and fails to address her attitude, he has failed to do his job—the job of reaching every listener—and has possibly opened the door to letting her undermine his message later with other staff members. Marcus doesn't have the power to change Sam's nature, but he has to let Sam know that he understands her and her concerns. He should anticipate subsequent conversations and pre-emptively deal with possible problems. When Marcus prepares for a staff meeting, analyzing Sam and every other member of his team is imperative.

Key Points

- Each audience is unique, so each speech must be unique. Build your message for each group. Even if your topic doesn't change from group to group, make sure the talk isn't generic and adjust your words to your audience.
- Think about the listeners. It is your job to get inside the heads of the audience members and understand as much about them as possible.
- Ask questions. Find out everything you can about the listeners. Spend time at the outset to learn about audience interests, characteristics, and biases. Don't ignore the obvious.
- Don't pretend to be someone you aren't. Adjust your words to be effective, not to fool the listeners.

2

Step 2: Content

Are you familiar with TED Talks? They began in 1984 with the purpose of spreading ideas. Speakers from many different fields talk for up to 20 minutes about education, technology, art, business, medicine, international relations, and more. TED Talks are enormously popular. So popular in fact that an offshoot, TEDx Talks, has sprung up around the country. Most speakers do not have name recognition—they have intriguing content. As an example, find a TEDx Talk by Shawn Achor, a "happiness researcher." In his talk, he manages to engage you with his opening story, make you laugh out loud, connect his ideas to your life, share a radical new way of thinking about workplace happiness, and give practical strategies for changing behavior—all in just 12 minutes. It's an impressive example of how to make a message valuable. Great content should be your goal, too.

Thinking About Content

Now that you understand your audience, what do you say to them? For many talks, some content is predetermined. In the workplace, trainers may have a handbook of material they have to cover, and are often given the slides, handouts, and badge requirements; educators may have to follow a set curriculum with textbooks and supporting materials; and managers may have information for employees that was handed down from someone else in the organization. It is tempting to take the generic material, cover all of it, and think the job is done, but how well does your audience receive the canned materials? You have probably experienced a mandatory listening situation and been unimpressed by that one-size-fits-all talk. Remember, just because the content was handed to you doesn't mean it was well made, and preprepared content is never sufficient. Even if most of what you have to say is required, delivering only that material is a mistake.

We often have more freedom once we move outside the workplace—wedding toasts, retirement dinners, and eulogies—but that freedom can often make things more difficult. We have to create all the content ourselves, and we may struggle trying to decide what to say. In this chapter, we'll look at ways to embellish content for prepackaged talks and create content for open-ended talks.

What's the Time Limit?

Let's start with the easiest content concept: Include only as much content as you can cover in the time allotted for your talk. Sometimes you'll be given the speech duration, so you'll know before you begin preparing that you are expected to speak for 20 minutes at the breakfast meeting, an hour on the webinar, 45 minutes at the conference, or six minutes at the wedding. Respect that time limit! Few people will be upset if you finish early; everyone will be upset if you go long. "I realize my time is up, but if I can have your attention for a few minutes more" are words the audience never wants to hear. Anything you say after the time limit has little impact, and every minute you continue beyond your given time risks audience hostility. A 10-minute stand-up meeting should be no longer than nine minutes and 59 seconds. Never violate this rule.

I have heard speakers lament that they "only have 45 minutes, but have to cover all this content!" so they race through the content in an attempt to respect the time limit. However, this is not the key to creating meaningful content. The problem is with the word *cover*. It's not a synonym for *unload*.

Can you cram two hours' worth of information into a 45-minute talk, training, or meeting? Sure, but know that your listeners will take in very little of what you say. Don't expose your listeners to a massive amount of information if you want them to understand and be influenced by your talk. No listeners retain 100 percent of what a speaker says, but if they feel overwhelmed, the retention percentage drops closer to zero. If you have two hours of content, but only 45 minutes to present it in, you need to cut an hour and 15 minutes of content. Figure out what you really need to get across. If the rest of the content is important, give it the time it deserves—but do it in another session or meeting.

Often the time limit is not specified. How long should this portion of the staff meeting be? How long should a eulogy, acceptance speech, or lecture on the importance of getting good grades be? One way to look at these questions is to consider attention span. There are a lot of different ideas about how long people can effectively listen, but a good rule of thumb is to think about yourself. How long do you pay attention? How long into the staff meeting can you pay attention before your mind wanders? What about a sermon or a TV show? Yes, our attention usually comes back after our minds wander, but for many listeners, total attention only lasts a short time and partial attention or inattention follows. Think about it: Television producers place commercial breaks into a show every seven minutes—how often do you find yourself reaching for your phone or computer to check your email or Instagram account right around the time the commercial break starts?

With this in mind, use seven to 12 minutes as a starting point for most talks when you're not given a specific time limit. If it's not possible to finish in that timeframe, consider offering listeners a break of some sort: Give them a couple of minutes to discuss, a moment to write down questions, an activity that helps them digest the message, and so on. Good speakers can easily hold attention for 20 minutes; great orators can hold attention for much longer. As you improve your speaking ability, you may extend the seven- to 12-minute window if necessary. But be very clear about this:

Effectiveness is lost if you speak without interruption for too long. Why keep talking if the audience has mentally left the room?

Why This Speech?

What is the purpose of your talk? To entertain? To inform? To motivate? To console? To warn? Sometimes the purpose is very clear. If you're training all your employees about the new EEOC requirements, the purpose is to inform. If you're handing out awards for the youth soccer season, it's to offer congratulations. If you're explaining online safety to your children, it's to inform and to caution. Knowing the purpose helps you determine what content to add. When explaining online safety, you might include facts about Internet privacy issues, the long-lasting nature of posts, the need to avoid online bullying, and then add an explanation of the consequences of violating the rules. The purpose of the speech directs much of its content.

Sometimes, it may not seem like there is a true purpose for your speech. What should you say at the bachelor or bachelorette party? The purpose of your toast is to amuse the audience and gently tease the groom- or bride-to-be. Tell stories that make clear what your relationship is and the great memories you created together. But you also need to think about how much teasing is appropriate and how explicit your story should be. Have you ever experienced a time where the speaker crossed a line during the toast? This makes the audience very uncomfortable and drains the fun. If you do your audience analysis well, you will know that some folks will be offended at things others find funny. Include only content that appeals to all listeners.

What about a commencement speech? Yes, the purpose is to honor the accomplishments of the graduates and inspire them about their futures, but the "trying your best," "the world needs you," and "reach for the stars" themes have all been played out. The purpose of a commencement speech is not to rattle off a bunch of clichés. Instead, think about adding personal stories about your life and offer your reflections about what graduation meant to you, and how that meaning changed over the years of your life.

What do you say at a funeral? Eulogies are about explaining the wonderful qualities of the deceased and how much the person meant to all those in attendance. Think about the stories, anecdotes, and quotes that reveal the character of the person. Were you co-workers? Add workplace stories. Were you leaders in the same church? Talk about the deceased in that context. Want to tell a humorous story? Use your audience analysis! Do listeners think this is a celebration of a fun life, or is it a tragic and somber remembrance? They are different purposes.

A Side Note About Stories

Storytelling is compelling, but only if the story is well chosen. Look for stories that drive home a key point and show rather than tell. For example, at a police officers' training session about community connection, you could include a story about a cop who used a radar gun to time little boys as they rode past on their bikes over and over, trying to set new records. Or a story about a beat cop who stopped to join a basketball game with a gang. Point out that these simple actions help to change people's perception of police from "people to fear" to "friends in the community."

At social events, look for stories that define the person. At my son's wedding, I wanted to let people know what kind of guy he is. I could have said, "Greg is a kind-hearted, thoughtful man." Instead, I told a story:

> *When Greg was six, his little brother broke one of his favorite toys. Greg was furious when he came to me. I said, "What would be a good punishment? Should you take one of his favorite toys and break it?" Greg started crying. "Noooo," he said. "Then Ross would feel as bad as I do now!"*

That story captures a character-revealing moment. Include this kind of story when you build your talks.

But you need to be careful. For stories to be effective, they must be concise. When we hear the word *story,* we think of the bedtime stories we loved as kids. Unfortunately, that leads many speakers to tell "once upon a time" stories that go on and on. What was the point of those bedtime stories? To put us to sleep. If you don't make your story short and to the point, you will have that same effect on your listeners.

Why You?

You were chosen for a reason. Maybe you are the subject matter expert, which means you know things that no listener knows. Your content will include that critical information, adjusted for the audience, of course, because they are not subject matter experts.

Or maybe you have a special relationship—father, mother, sibling, best friend of the bride-to-be, old college buddy, longtime co-worker—and you were chosen because you have stories and memories no one else has. Your content should include those special stories. Don't make the mistake made by the father of the bride at another wedding I attended. He gave a toast that anyone could have given—best wishes and a couple of inspirational quotes. There was absolutely nothing to indicate that he knew either of the two people just married. No story of his little girl growing up? No story about first meeting his new son-in-law? A huge mistake. Personalize your message.

Maybe you have special qualities. Perhaps you were chosen for your sense of humor, storytelling ability, unique perspective, or special experiences. If this is true, make sure your content demonstrates this. Caution: Make sure your words fit your personality. Don't try to do what you cannot. Should you include a joke because you read somewhere that humor is good for speeches? Not unless you are known for humor. For example, my business partner's wife cannot tell a joke. It's hard to figure out where it goes wrong, but a joke that gets laughs when told by someone else dies when she tells it. She is a nice person, but she is not a funny person. Be yourself. It is fine to watch great speakers and get ideas for improving your speaking, but don't mimic them. Talk like you.

And Yet It Isn't About You

The biggest mistake speakers make is thinking that talks are about what they want to say. No presentation is about what the speaker wants to say. All talks must be audience-based: What works for the listeners? Focus on them, not on you.

I was once asked by a large publishing company to speak in Egypt. The local representative was supposed to say a few words about the company and then introduce me. The agenda allotted 15 minutes for his talk. He used 35, spending most of that time detailing his ascent from a refugee camp in Jordan to a job at a chicken restaurant to an executive at a publishing company. He deserved to be proud of himself, but the occasion was not about him. Many speakers make the same mistake to some extent. We have something we want to say and we don't pay enough attention to when the message goes offtrack.

Successful talks are not simply about saying what is right for the occasion; they are about what the audience can get out of them. Think of training sessions you have been a part of in which attendees made subtle eye contact with each other and gave an "Isn't this just the worst?" expression. Or think of the times parents have prattled on and on to teenage children, telling the kids all the things they want to say as the children roll their eyes, dismissing all of it. Just because you want to cover it, doesn't mean the audience will care. Just because you want to say it, doesn't mean the audience will be able to receive it. Always focus on making sure your listeners are on board, before focusing on where you want the train to go. And be careful: You may be fascinated by the topic, but the audience may not share your interest. It is the job of the speaker to make the content work for the audience.

To review: You added just enough content to fill the time allotted, you added content appropriate for the purpose, and you added your personal touches. To make a truly exceptional talk requires a bit more, though. With some thoughtful additions to your content, you can build an impressive and compelling message.

One Size Does Not Fit All

As a gag gift, a friend of mine gave me a product she saw advertised on television. I'll describe it as a cross between a blanket and a robe. On the box was the claim "One size fits all." Picture a Green Bay Packer lineman and a Kentucky Derby jockey. Guess what: There is no "garment" that would fit both of them, and my blanket with sleeves probably doesn't exactly fit anyone.

There is no talk that fits everyone either. A common mistake trainers and educators make is believing that because the message doesn't change, the talk doesn't need to change. The insurance procedures don't change from office to office, for example, so just show up and deliver your content, right? Wrong. One size fits none. Here's how to tailor content to fit your audience, whether that audience is one person or many.

Adjusting Vocabulary and Grammar

When I ask people what is needed to be a great speaker, I often hear, "Good speakers have great vocabularies!" and "Great speakers use good grammar." I disagree. Grammar and vocabulary need to match the audience and occasion. When my teammate walked into the dugout and said, "I ain't mad atcha," no one corrected him and suggested that he say, "I am not angry with you." His language was perfectly fine for that occasion, and breaking grammar rules was not a problem. On the other hand, at a job interview for a management position at a consulting firm, I'd recommend proper grammar and high-level but natural vocabulary. At a talk for Parents' Jobs Day in a third-grade classroom, you need to make yet another kind of vocabulary adjustment.

We do audience analysis to determine vocabulary and grammar. Feel free to couch your content in language appropriate for the situation if that is what comes naturally for you.

What about profanity? If you go to a comedy club, you'll probably hear language that would be shocking if you heard it in a church. But at the comedy club, profanity works. We all play the game of "Is it OK to swear?" when talking to people we just met. At some point, a tentative "Wow, that was a . . . hell of a serve" comes out, and we think to ourselves, "Oh, it will be acceptable if I reply, 'Damn straight!'" In individual conversation, it is reasonable to match the language of the person with whom you are talking. You don't have to speak like a sailor if it makes you uncomfortable, but in some situations, you could if you'd like. What about group situations? If there's a chance someone will be offended, then why take the risk? Keep your audience comfortable and control your words.

Adding Clarifying Content

Eschew obfuscation. Some readers may wonder what that means. If so, I have some explaining to do. Good speakers make sure the listeners never spend time wondering, "What does that mean?" You should be aware of your listeners and anticipate where explaining will be needed. Always think about whether you need to add clarifying content to make your message clear. I was once told that a new directive from ESC required us to include CSAPs and RIT scores on the IEPs and 504s. Some may know what that means, but your goal as a speaker is to make sure all listeners understand. Do you need to add some definitions because you as the expert know things the audience doesn't? Do you need to explain some circumstances so they understand the situation? Do you need to set the stage for them because they were not involved in earlier events? These kinds of content additions may be necessary to ensure that you and the audience are on the same page. Your audience will not be happy if you have inside jokes that only a few people get or references to events that most people missed. Explain. Make sure every audience member understands every part of your message.

Sometimes you have to familiarize your audience about a topic to enable you to do your teaching. I talked to a teacher in Dubai who told me she was asking her students to read a book about Jackie Robinson. But I didn't realize until she pointed it out—that before teaching the story, she had to teach her students about baseball and about race relations in the United States. This teaching before the teaching took a lot of time, but without it, no child would understand the story. What do you have to teach your audience before you share your message? And even though the message is the same, you may have to add nothing in one location, while in another you may have to add a lot. Prepare your audience so they can be receptive.

Keeping Your Audience's Attention

Some talks are naturally interesting. The retelling of the vacation when Uncle Bob was dancing on the table at Carlos and Charlie's after eight margaritas has some intrinsic interest. Unfortunately, not every talk keeps our attention like that one. When I was a teacher, I attended a meeting in which a person from the district office was going from school to school to train teachers about how to proctor the annual state assessment exam. Her enormous list of procedures about how to hand out the tests, collect the tests, secure the tests, color in the circles, read the directions, time the sections, and so on, fascinated no one. Almost everyone quit paying attention within 10 minutes.

In fairness, hers was not a fascinating topic. She was chosen for her special knowledge of the procedures, and she explained the procedures to us, so she did exactly what she was supposed to do, right? Wrong. Although the speech must include certain things, including only those things is not sufficient. Speakers who present topics they know are dry should work especially hard to go beyond the minimal content and ensure that there is something to make the speech interesting. Yes, that can be difficult for some occasions, such as test-proctor training, but it can be done. She could have added an amusing anecdote about a situation in the school in which test proctoring went wrong. She should have varied slide designs to break up the monotony. She should have included some activity to rekindle audience interest. Given that folks start to mentally wander, check emails, text, and so on after seven to 12 minutes, a good speaker prepares for that and adds things in the speech to bring the audience back.

Adding Connectors

Great speakers connect with their audience. They take whatever topic they have and make listeners believe that the talk was designed just for them. Connectors are statements that directly relate to the audience, make it clear the speaker understands them and where they are coming from, and that prove audience analysis was well done.

Connecting With the Audience

When I work with people around the country and around the world, I realize that I am an outsider. Audience members think "Who is this guy?"

and "Why should I listen to him?" and so on. These are fair questions, and all speakers get some version of these. Employees think managers are on the other side of the "us versus them" line. That is inevitable in any hierarchical situation. Children think parents are out of touch, and parental comments do not apply to them. Teachers in Cairo can't immediately see how someone who only has experience teaching in the United States can relate to them in Egypt. You need to break through these barriers and find ways to connect with the listeners.

Did you know that Fort Wayne, Indiana, has a professional baseball team? A few steps below the major leagues, the Fort Wayne TinCaps play Single A ball at Parkview Field. How do I know? When I was working with an organization in Fort Wayne, I picked up a local paper at the airport and looked for information about the city. During my talk, I made a couple of comments about the team, which resulted in an immediate positive response. At another training session, I used food as a connector. I asked someone at the hotel for a dinner recommendation the night before, and then I used her recommendation the next day: "Hey, it's time for lunch. Who's going to Casa del Sol?" That started a fun conversation about Mexican restaurants, and I moved from outsider to part of the group: "He took time to learn about our community? We like him!"

Another simple but effective technique includes finishing these sentence starters with knowledge from your local audience:

- I know you have all been to . . .
- What I am telling you now is sort of like what you all do when . . .
- I have kids, too, and like yours, sometimes those kids . . .
- Let's face it, not everyone thinks like you do about this.
  I know you believe . . .
- Earlier, a member of your group was telling me about
  when you . . .
- I know you love golf. This is like being on the first tee at
  the Masters . . .
- Let me tell you a story about [*name of someone in audience who
  you got permission to talk about*] . . .

- I realize this may affect you differently than others because you . . .
- I was a teenager once, too. I remember when I did . . .
- Did you see the story in the paper today about . . . ?
- I've often wondered about [*topic*]. Have you?

Other ideas include adding an inside joke that only this group would get, or changing a story to make it specific to your audience. It can be as simple as changing "Did you hear the story about the accountant who was golfing in a lightning storm?" to "Did you hear the story about the HR manager who was golfing in a lightning storm?" Perhaps you throw in some names of audience members that you picked up as you talked with them before the session: "Jared and Olivia were saying earlier that. . . ."

The goal is to let the audience know that you are talking *with* them rather than talking *at* them. If you care enough to tailor your remarks to fit the group, the listeners will care enough to listen. Sometimes you will need several connectors. If an audience has several subgroups, add something for each one. At the high school awards banquet, you should say some things specifically for the honorees, but you would be wise to acknowledge the parents in attendance, too. A moving eulogy will mention all the things the deceased meant to the family, as well as all he meant to co-workers, friends, teammates, and anyone else in attendance. Every time you speak, make specific statements to connect yourself to the listener.

Connecting the Topic to the Audience

Why am I here? What does this have to do with me? It isn't always obvious to our listeners why they should care. Perhaps your financial firm requires the OSHA Universal Precautions training about how to deal with bodily fluids in the workplace. Employees may be questioning the purpose, thinking that at no time in their work history has anyone ever split their head open in their cubicle or thrown up on their desk. Presenting a new sales strategy for selling more ties with shirts? The top salesman for the region may not think he needs a new strategy. What about the parent who gives a safety lecture about driving to all her children after one of them got in a car accident? The ones who never got into a wreck will be miffed at being lectured to. No doubt you have your own examples of times you felt a topic didn't apply to you. As a speaker, make sure your listeners understand why your message is important for them.

Cutting the Fat

Content is not only about what needs to be included. We also need to discuss what needs to be excluded. Remember Everett's poor emcee skills? Every year he told us the complete history of the awards banquet. Turns out a committee was formed in April 1996, and consisted of three people: Walt Schmidt, Carol Montgomery, and David Lopez. I'm sure they were nice people, but the audience was not interested in a history lesson.

Digressions are a huge problem for many speakers—eliminate them. What else needs to be cut? Extraneous information. Give the audience only what they need to know. Get rid of nonessential information:

> *The new rules were decided upon on June 3 last year.*

> *As I was driving last Tuesday or Wednesday maybe—no, it was Tuesday. Anyhow I was on Highway 47 just 12 or 13 miles east of Scottsbluff close to the turnoff for Gering, and I had this thought.*

The first sentence contains information no one cares about and no one will remember. The second sentence has too many details, which may cause audience members to drift away.

Eliminating Verbal Viruses

There is another kind of nonessential content, something I call a "verbal virus." Unfortunately, verbal viruses seem to spread. Phrases such as "you know," "OK?" "know what I'm sayin'," "right?" and the ubiquitous "like" infect speaking. How many times have you heard them?

> *We are all going to have to, like, follow these new procedures. We, like, have to ring up the sale this way, and if a customer, like, says he wants a refund, then . . .*

I want to tell you about the new procedures, OK? We will now ring up the sale this way, OK? We can still give a discount, though, OK?

We are going to have to work on this. Know what I'm sayin'? She didn't like the first version so I added a part. Know what I'm sayin'?

By now new viruses may have infected speech, but the problem is the same.

Nothing diminishes speaker respect more than these words or phrases. If you want to be taken seriously, cure these viruses and eliminate these phrases.

Eliminating Pet Phrases, Big Words, and Jargon

Some speakers seem to have favorite phrases. I have a friend who interjects "if you will" into everything he says:

I went to the store to buy a new computer, if you will. I knew what I wanted. The manager showed me several models, but some of them were refurbished, if you will. I didn't want a refurbished computer; I wanted a new one.

In my opinion, audiences have a hard time, if you will, listening to your pet phrase. Record yourself. In my opinion, you should count the number of times, if you will, that a phrase occurs. If I may say so, I think you should eliminate, if you will, any phrase you use more than twice. In my opinion, audiences notice these things and, if I may say so, will hate listening to them.

Sometimes speakers try to change language in a "speaking" situation. They think a "speech" has to use fancy words and that big words impress. My friend Andre always substitutes a big word for a simple word:

Josh indicated to me that . . .

Indicated to me? Josh told me. That's sufficient. And who decided that *utilize* should be utilized in every situation where *use* would work just as well? Don't overutilize a big word where a perfectly good small word can be utilized instead. Listeners don't want you to wear out their ears trying to utilize that thesaurus you got. (See how tiring that gets?)

Finally, never use jargon or acronyms. Every business has its own special language:

> Leaving ADDIE for SAM *involves using SMEs to share ISD strategies.*

Yes, some people in the audience are in the business and can decipher the acronyms effortlessly, but others will have to think about it, which is distracting, and many will simply tune out.

Every word in the speech must have a specific purpose. The basic content plus clarifiers plus something to hold interest plus connectors minus verbal viruses, fat, and jargon—that is what makes a successful talk. If you can't tell why something in the speech is necessary, cut it.

Key Points

- You were chosen for a reason. Use your uniqueness. You are special, so make sure the audience knows what is special about you. Include your personal stories and let your personality show through your words.
- You have a purpose. Say what you are supposed to say. Cover the topic you are supposed to cover and don't get offtrack.
- Add content to clarify and explain. Think of what the audience knows, not just what you know. Include information essential to making sure your audience understands your message. The listener should never be thinking, "I don't know what she is talking about."
- Include attention-holding elements.
- Connect with the audience by tailoring remarks specifically for them. Make it clear that you understand them and are talking to them, not some generic audience.

- Avoid verbal viruses. "Like," "You know," and "Right?" are annoying and should be avoided.
- Don't overuse a phrase. Check to make sure you don't have a habit of saying something too often.
- Cut the jargon. Every profession has its own special language, but that language becomes tiresome to listeners.
- Use simple words. Never use a large word when a small word will do the job just as well.

Step 3: Organization

Before a tournament at my grandson's martial arts academy, the sensei gave a talk. Here's what I think he did: He got 100 strips of paper. On some of them, he wrote down every athletic cliché he could think of. On several, every all-American cliché he knew. On a few, some information about his past accomplishments. On others, all the ways martial arts might be good for children. And on the rest, some random facts about his family. He put them all into a basket and mixed them up, then randomly pulled them out and read each one aloud.

It was one of the most distinctive talks I have ever heard, but it was not a good talk. I'm sure he made some important points in there somewhere, but the sheer randomness of their presentation was mind-boggling. I presume he has a disciplined approach to many aspects of his life, but the lack of discipline in organizing his ideas ruined the impact of his talk.

Organizational Basics

Your talk is designed specifically for your listeners, and you have all the content needed for a memorable one. Now you have to organize that content. Where do you start? How do you finish? How do you tie all the pieces together?

Almost all books about speaking suggest you should tell us what you are going to say, say it, and then tell us what you said. It's a cliché, but it works. It provides a beginning, middle, and end, and lets the listeners know exactly what to expect. For example:

> *Today I will tell you a couple of funny stories about Armando's early years. Then I will tell you the three reasons why I think Armando should get this award because he really does deserve it.*
>
> *Let me start with the funny stories. When Armando was first hired. . . . That's not the only time he got into trouble. He also . . .*
>
> *But let's get to the main reason we are here. Armando deserves this award because he always. . . . The second reason why we chose Armando is because. . . . Finally, Armando is the kind of guy who. . . . That's why he is here tonight.*
>
> *So now you know about the early Armando years, and you know why he is the man of the hour. Congratulations, Armando.*

The formula is based on a simple truth: People do not listen well. Listeners do a better job of getting the message when they know what's coming. To aid your listeners, you should make it very clear what they will need to listen for during the speech, and then you need to remind them immediately about what they have just heard to reinforce the message. That's why this formula is a reasonable starting place for organizing a speech, despite its commonness.

Beyond the Cliché

Of course, saying it is a starting place suggests that there is more to do. Let's add some elements to move your talk from ordinary to exceptional. It doesn't matter whether you have an audience of one or 1,000, or whether they are listening to you in person or through digital media. You still need to organize a talk around these things: a grabber opening, a purposeful method of organizing, signposts, and a powerful closing.

Make a Great First Impression

It takes 385 seconds for an interviewer to decide if a candidate is right for the job. Employers say work experience is the number one factor in hiring someone for a position, but first impressions come in second (Zolfaghar-ifard 2014). That is a cautionary note for those searching for jobs, but it is also instructive for speakers. First impressions matter. Regardless of whom you are talking to or what you are talking about, you must have an opening that grabs the listener's attention, turning initial polite attentiveness into prolonged interest.

Often, speakers start a speech with, "Hi. My name is Lin Chen, and I want to say a few words about . . ." But, "My name is . . ." should never be your opening words. If listeners don't already know who you are, introduce yourself, but share your name after some engaging opening:

> *800 million people are starving on this planet. 800 million. We have food, but we just can't get it to the people in need. I'm Lin Chen, director of Feed the Planet.*

Grab interest, then introduce. That principle works for all talks.

> *Today we are going to learn about instructional design.*

Boring. Try this instead.

> *Look at this slide. Dreadful. Dull. And, unfortunately, typical. You might create one of these monsters. Well, you might have without this training. Today we are going to improve instructional design.*

Much better, right? Open your talk well. The following are just a few ways to hook listeners. Use them or something similar. Do not simply begin speaking.

The Challenge

Some speeches are designed to motivate listeners, asking for money or time or help.

I am going to ask you to do something difficult, something few people have ever done.

This immediately intrigues the listener.

Today, we have a chance to make a huge difference.

This engages listeners and makes them wonder what they will be called upon to do.

The Unexpected Statement

My wife, Anne, is an Olympic gold medalist, and she is occasionally called upon to speak about her experiences. She opens with:

Don't root for America's heroes. Don't root for the athletes you see in advertisements or the athletes that you read about in the press.

Highly unexpected, isn't it? The audience is inevitably curious and begins to pay attention after a shocking statement like that. Don't worry. She goes on to talk about how demanding the training is for all the athletes at the Games and how impressive it is to be 10th in the entire world, just 0.4 seconds behind the gold medalist. She suggests that the audience ought to root for *all* the athletes and honor *all* the accomplishments, and not succumb to hero worshiping only athletes who have won or are expected to win several medals.

She finishes by modifying her opening statement:

So don't just root for the names the network has been pushing. Root for them and root for all the others, too. Don't just watch America's stars; also watch the world's stars.

The audience was with her all the way because the opening was so unexpected.

The Poignant Story

Sometimes it is appropriate to open with a story that grabs the listeners' hearts. This is especially true if your purpose is to persuade the audience.

Politicians know this, so when they introduce new legislation for a jobs bill, they start with a story:

> *Meet this poor family: The husband lost his job; the family lost their health insurance; little Joey could not get treatment for asthma.*

People raising money for a cause can make the need for donations clear with a story about the recipients' plight. Engage hearts, and you will engage your audience.

Involve an Audience Member

I love to start with a story about someone in the audience, someone everyone knows. I always get permission ahead of time, and I use the information I got from my audience research. If I overhear something as I talk to the event organizer, I latch on to it. Karen just got engaged? I don't know Karen, but I include her story.

> *Let me tell you what happened to Karen last week. Did you know that her fiancé asked her to look at the Jumbotron after the fourth quarter? Well, I'm guessing that he proposed not because of her many great qualities but because he knew she was going to attend this training and become a master at coaching her colleagues.*

Instantly, the audience is on your side. They know you took the time to get to know them, and they love hearing about one of their own.

Humorous Anecdote

Most people like to laugh. If you have an on-point, humorous story, you can use it to relax the audience and get them on your side. Maybe you have a personal anecdote about an event in your life: "Last week, my son came home from school and . . ." Maybe you picked up a funny story from someone the audience is familiar with: "George Carlin noticed that 'a scary dream makes your heart beat faster. Why doesn't the part of your brain that controls your heartbeat realize that another part of your brain is making the whole thing up? Don't these people communicate?' Today will focus on how to improve our communication skills to avoid similar problems" (Carlin 1997).

Don't open with a joke just to tell a joke unless you are doing stand-up comedy. Tell a story that fits the occasion. And don't tell a humorous story unless you can tell a good one. Some people are terrible storytellers. Recall my business partner's wife from the last chapter. Only use a humorous anecdote if you often make people around you laugh.

A Great Quote

A quotation can make the audience think. If the quote is from a powerful person, the speaker can instantly command respect. "Ronald Reagan once said . . ." followed by connecting the quote to the business at hand makes for a dramatic and thought-provoking beginning to your speech. But remember, never use a quotation from a person the audience will not recognize. I have heard speakers say something like, "According to Herman Smudzinski, 'No organization can survive if. . . .'" Herman who? If we don't know the man, the quote loses power.

The Shocking Fact

Shocking facts are great for grabbing the audience.

> *Only one of eight children attending Trevista Elementary School will graduate from high school. One out of eight.*

Listeners will want to hear more. Why is that true? Can that be changed? This is an effective opening when your goal is to motivate listeners to solve a problem.

The Teaser

Commercials have used teasers for a long time: "Want to lose weight fast?" "Want to save time and money?" The commercials don't say it, but we hear it: Well then, just listen to what I am about to say. The same sort of trick will work for you, too. "I'm going to tell you something that will save you thousands of dollars" or "Before this speech is over, you will learn something few people ever learn." Of course, then you must deliver. Before you finish, you better include a money-saving tip or share something unique.

Organizing the Main Content

Now that you have the audience's interest, how do you decide what story to share first, what lesson to begin with, or what policy to explain when? Unloading a jumble of ideas is not ideal. Listeners need some structure. Some speeches suggest structure, while others allow more options. These are useful ways to organize.

Chronological or Sequential

If your speech involves explaining the steps of a process or a project timeline, the organization takes care of itself. Start at the beginning and proceed to the end. It would be quite odd to hear a speaker describe step five and then go back to steps two and three, or for an instructor to say, "Fill in line 23 on the form with the correct amount. But before you fill in line 23, make sure you read the directions to step 11 and add lines 11 and 12 together."

You wouldn't expect to hear about what happened in August before you heard about what happened in May. Tell your story in the proper order if things happen sequentially.

Problem and Solution

If you want to explain a problem and then introduce a solution, start with the problem. Before the tech specialist tells me how to adjust my computer's security settings, she should tell me what the problems are with the current settings. Before you introduce the new organizational structure, tell listeners what was wrong with the old one. Before you ground your daughter, explain what the problems were with her behavior.

The Acronym

An acronym can be a very effective memory tool to help recall important points. They can also be powerful mnemonic tools. Can you name the colors of the rainbow? I bet you thought of Roy G. Biv. I grew up in the Midwest, and we remember the names of the Great Lakes because of HOMES.

The same principle can work in speeches to help the audience organize and remember your ideas. In a safety presentation, you may tell miners to use the SLAM method:

- Stop and think through the task.
- Look and identify hazards.
- Analyze whether you have the proper training for the task.
- Manage by removing or controlling the hazards.

A school lunchroom has CURB:

- Clean up after yourself.
- Use your table voice.
- Raise your hand.
- Be safe and respectful.

Does your company have a poster in the break room with an acronym? Has a trainer or manager introduced a new program that applies to your job and left behind a poster with an acronym as a reminder? Acronyms can be great, but let me offer a caution: Listeners can be buried in acronyms. At a training conference last May, I saw xAPI, 4Cs map, RSVP, LLAMA, SCORE, MOOCs, VUCA, BYOD, and PLA, just to name a few. If you're concerned that another acronym will put your audience over the edge and make them wish for BYOB, don't force it.

Geographical Area

Sometimes the subject matter can be organized by regions, either geographically or by areas within a location. Instead of just dumping a lot of information on the listeners in a random fashion, try grouping the information by location.

Let's look at the sales in the Northeast, the Southeast, the Midwest, and then the Mountain States.

Let's look at the sales in women's wear, men's wear, children's, and finally, home furnishings.

Circular

Remember the speech my wife gave about not rooting for America's stars? After the body of the speech, she brought the audience back to the line she opened with:

> *So let me repeat. Do not root for America's heroes. Don't root for the athletes you see in advertisements or the athletes that you read about in the press. Instead, root for all . . .*

That is one use of circular organization: Bring us back to the opening statement.

A repeating process also forces us to use circular organization:

> *We will evaluate the solutions we have available to us. Here is how we'll do that . . . Based on that evaluation, we will select a strategy. A committee will be formed to choose the strategy that . . . Then we will collect data. We will monitor 12 criteria. Based on the data we collect, we will evaluate the strategy's effectiveness and once more evaluate the solutions available to us.*

The talk naturally takes us back to the beginning.

Parallel Structure

Parallel structure is powerful. It works well if you have a list of things to say. For example, I once heard a speaker talk about the health benefits of exercise:

> *Exercise does three things for you. It helps you lose weight. You can avoid diseases. Many people find it increases their energy.*

His message would have been more powerful if he had used parallel form: starting each of his points with the same couple of words.

> *Exercise enables you to lose weight. Exercise enables you to avoid diseases. Exercise enables you to maintain energy.*

> *You can lose weight. You can avoid diseases. You can increase energy.*

Consistent phrasing from one sentence to the next aids memory.

You can also use parallel structure to set off sections of your speech. Perhaps the greatest example of this is Martin Luther King Jr.'s "I Have a Dream" speech. We all remember his repetition of phrases. In one section of the speech, he repeats, "We can never be satisfied . . ."; in another, he repeats, "One hundred years later . . ."; and of course, in the final section he repeats, "I have a dream today. . . ." His phrasing lets us know we have entered a different section of the speech.

Alphabetical

Use the alphabet to organize your thoughts. If you can, put items in alphabetical order for discussion:

> *Let's look at our recent contracts. We will look at the Davis contract, the Jeffries contract, the Neilson contract, and the Rynd contract.*

Be careful to avoid forcing an alphabetical pattern:

> *Today, we will talk about our new ABC program. First, Attend the developmental meetings. Next, ideas for new products should be Brought to the Committee for product development. Next week, we'll discuss LMNO!*

If it doesn't fit, don't force it.

Compare and Contrast

A compare and contrast speech allows for a different organizational structure. It's usually a list of similarities followed by a list of differences. What if you're comparing the old procedures and the new procedures, or explaining the features of two different products? Instead of describing all the details of one and then describing all the details of the other, it would be easier to group the similarities and differences:

> *To help you decide between the Axiom 950 and the Axiom 960, let me explain the features. Both have auto shutoff, low flow sperving vents. . . . So, in many ways they are the same. There are some differences, though. The 950 has an AC adaptor, but the 960 does not. The 950 has an HDMI cord only, but the 960 has an HDMI cord and a USB3 cord . . .*

Order of Importance

Sometimes speakers have several points to make. I caution you to whittle down that number of points. If you try to share more than three points, you will discover that audience members remember no points. Listeners do not walk away with all 14 of your great ideas in their heads. You would prefer they remember three out of three points rather than a random one or two from a larger number, wouldn't you? So, after deciding which three key points the audience absolutely must get, open with the second-best point and finish with the best point. (This is another chance to use your audience analysis: What would this group think is the best reason or most important idea?) Audiences recall the beginning better than the middle, and they recall the ending better than either of those.

Related Ideas

This applies to topical speeches in which the speaker is asked to focus on ideas that are somehow related. For example, I was once asked to speak about which 21st-century skills should be taught in schools to ensure that students are prepared for the workplace. I began with a discussion of collaboration skills, moved to a discussion of Internet literacy skills, then continued with a discussion of web publishing skills, and so on. There was no particular order needed, as long as I grouped like ideas together and was clear about moving from one group to the next.

Signposts

It's reassuring to know where you are in a journey and how far you are from your destination. Visualize the last trip you took on a highway. Remember those green signs along the road—"Denver 118 miles" and "Denver 94 miles" and "Denver 67 miles" and finally "Denver next 6 exits"? They keep you aware of where you are and where you are going. Listeners love signposts in a talk: explicitly stated verbal markers telling them where they are and where they are headed.

Recall that cliché for organizing a speech: Tell us what you are going to say, say it, and then tell us what you said. It is really just a form of signage, a way to let your audience know where you're going, where you are now, and where you have been. Speakers often resist the idea of including obvious markers because they think inserting signposts is awkward. The truth is, though, that most people need listening aids, and they'll get more out of a speech if they have specific signposts along the way. At the basic level, signposts are numeric. For example:

> *There will be some challenges ahead. I believe the three most important obstacles to overcome are logistical issues, attitudinal issues, and language issues. First, let's look at logistical issues. How can we set up the room to accommodate 600 attendees? How can we get sufficient Internet access? How can we feed everyone? Second, let's look at the attitudinal issues. Some of the attendees are likely to be opposed to the change we are going to propose. Others will be enthusiastic supporters. We have to bring everyone along. Third, let's look at the language issues. Attendees are coming from several different countries.*

Although using first, second, and third is not sophisticated, it is more effective than not being specific about how your speech is organized. The listeners are notified at the outset to be looking for three challenges, and because the challenges are well marked they do not need to wonder whether what they just heard was one of them. This also makes the challenges easier to recall at the end of the speech.

Once a speaker reaches a more advanced level, signposts become more fluid:

> *There will be great challenges ahead and you will all have to face these challenges. But I believe three challenges are more important than the rest. To begin, there are. . . . In addition, we have to. . . . Finally, . . .*

In a talk for a special occasion, the speaker might say:

> *But enough about the college years. Consider those early years on the job. Holly was always quick to. . . . And after those early years on the job? Well, Holly mastered every aspect of the business and developed key relationships with. . . . Key relationships aside, Holly has always impressed me with her key traits. . . .*

In this situation, the speaker subtly yet clearly told us he was moving from the college years to Holly's early years with the company, and then on to her ability to form relationships, and finally to her best traits. He was able to present a variety of information without jumbling it up into a confusing mess. Be explicit in stating the signposts—don't make the audience wonder where this is all going.

Powerful Closings

Once you finish the body of the speech, you must build a conclusion. I've heard far too many speeches end awkwardly, where the speaker just stopped talking. This leaves the audience in limbo. Is it really over? Your talk must avoid that problem.

The ending of your talk needs to be obvious and dynamic. One option is the one in the cliché—tell us what you told us—where you simply reiterate or highlight the main points. In this case, the speech ending is summative:

> *To conclude, I want to review my four reasons for national healthcare: to eliminate waste, to save money, to help the poor, and to save lives.*

This accomplishes half of the job of a great ending—it is obvious. At least the listeners know the situation.

But the other half of the job is to be dynamic. Let's look at a few ways great speakers wrap up their talks.

Leave the listeners with one memorable thought or key, unforgettable concept:

> *Five Solomon Islands are now under water. Five. The problem isn't off in the distance. It is here. Now.*

End with a rhetorical question that clearly ends the speech, but causes the audience to continue thinking:

> *Somewhere in America, a child will die today due to a lack of healthcare. If we do nothing, the deaths will continue. Can you live with that?*

Finish with a call to action:

> *We cannot sit back and let our school continue to get hurt by lack of funding. We all have to sign the petition. We must hit the phones. We need to go door-to-door to get out the vote!*

End with a personal anecdote. If it is on point, a good anecdote can guarantee the audience is on your side:

> *But I don't want to talk about the season in general. Let me tell you why I consider this to be one of my favorite seasons. It was the third game of the season, and we were behind. Annette had been injured the week before and couldn't play, but she was on the sideline with us. When the team came over for a timeout, Annette did something that explains why I love coaching and why I love this team. She. . . .*

Use an opening for your closing. Some of the ideas for great openings we discussed at the start of this chapter also make a powerful closing. Try ending your talk with a challenge, a humorous story, or a quote.

> *I challenge you to eliminate all safety violations and set the record for accident-free workdays.*

Just remember: Under no circumstances should a speech simply stop.

Key Points

- Open with a grabber. Immediately command the audience's attention and engage their minds. Take their initial curiosity and give them a reason to continue listening.
- Organize your words. Don't ramble on without a plan. Pick the right type of organizational strategy.
- Use signposts. Make sure the listeners always know exactly where you are and where you are headed. Be specific and obvious with your markers—don't assume the audience can figure out the structure. Tell them exactly.

- Finish strong and leave an impression. Don't make the audience guess whether you have finished. Choose a powerful and memorable closing.

Step 4: Looks

I once got to work with some trainers at Climax Molybdenum Mine near Leadville, Colorado. I usually wear a suit, dress shirt, and tie, or a sport coat and a dress shirt when I work.

Do you think I dressed in my usual way for the job at the mine? No. I didn't think steel-toed boots, a requirement at the site, would go well with any of my suits. Instead I decided that jeans and a down vest were more reasonable, especially because part of the training session involved tromping around outside in October at an altitude of 11,000 feet. Interestingly, that's what many of the trainees were wearing, too. Aside from my brand-new boots, I looked like many of them. Make no mistake, looks are important.

Choosing the Right Look

When you go to a job interview, you probably give a lot of thought about (and may even agonize over) how to dress: "Should I wear this?" "Is this a suit and tie company?" "Does this make me look professional?" I bet you go through the same kind of thinking as you get ready for a wedding: "How formal is this event?" "What are other people wearing?" "Is this a good color on me?" "Will this tie go with your dress?"

In these situations, you want to fit in, you want to be appropriately dressed, and you hope people will think you look good. Giving a talk is no different! Make sure you plan your appearance before every speech. "How you dress" may seem like an odd addition to a book about creating a speech, but the minute you arrive people will begin judging you based on the look you created. This is true whether you are leading a sales meeting, training new haul truck drivers, or telling the soccer team how to run a set piece.

Visualize the following situations: candidates at a debate, executives at big tech companies speaking at new product rollouts, teachers meeting parents at back to school night, and coaches on the softball field. What are people wearing? There is a certain look that fits each place. The same is true of every situation in which you will be speaking. Your style of dress changes the audience's perception of you, and you certainly don't want to start off by making a negative impression.

You've already analyzed the audience so that you could tailor your talk to them. Use what you learned to help you figure out which outfit will create the biggest impact. Are they formal? Casual? Try to match their style. Then think about your purpose and your position. Are you leading a training session or heading out to an after-work get together? Are you headed to a workplace where tattoos and purple hair are ideal, or one where they need to be covered? Showing up to an interview at IBM in jeans and a T-shirt is just as absurd as wearing a tuxedo to the scout meeting. In situations where you aren't sure, always err on the formal side. It is better to be a bit more formal than your listeners rather than a bit less formal.

Additionally, avoid distracting clothing that will annoy your listeners. (We'll talk more about this in the chapter on poise.) I can't emphasize enough how important it is to wear a comfortable, well-fitting outfit. I have watched speakers adjust straps that were coming out, tug at collars that were too tight, hitch up pants that were too big, and suck in stomachs trying to fit into sport coats that were too small. These may seem innocuous, but they often make the audience uncomfortable. You should also be sure to dress in layers, because, indoors or out, the temperature can be capricious. You don't want to be sweating or shivering because the air-conditioning is not functioning correctly or a breeze came up. Wear an outfit that can be adjusted for conditions. And you may heat up as you talk. The suit jacket that seemed comfortable at first may seem warm once you get going. You can't control sweating, but you can dress to minimize it.

And it's not just what you're wearing that can distract the audience. I have seen speakers with half of their faces covered by bangs or hair that falls over one side of their face. In addition to hiding their faces from the audience (a bad idea), such hairstyles lead to annoying head jerks or a constant hand-tucking-the-hair-back-behind-the-ear gesture as the speakers try to get the hair off their faces and out of their eyes. Don't show up on performance day without a hair band or barrette.

Finally, know that changing your style of dress changes your attitude. Do you have an outfit that makes you feel great? A power suit or a lucky red dress? When I started to lead more training sessions for different groups around the world and give keynotes at conventions, my wife suggested that I spend more money on clothes. I resisted at first, saying "But that's not who I am! I don't normally do this." Then I gave in and let her get me a new suit to wear for a talk in New York. I realized how good her suggestion was when I noticed that everyone in the audience had business-formal dress. And I noticed something else: The suit changed my attitude. I felt more powerful, more in control of the situation. You may be giving some talks you never thought you would be doing either. Perhaps you're an air-conditioning repair person who has been tasked with training every repair person in your company. Or maybe you've been told to train your team about social media, even though you're the youngest member. You should dress to impress…you! Your clothes can make you feel confident and impressive, which in turn will help you be more confident and impressive.

Key Points

- Looks matter. Listeners will notice what you are wearing and make judgments.
- Your style of dress should be appropriate for the audience and occasion. Be as well dressed or slightly better dressed than they are.
- Wear well-fitting clothes that don't distract you or your listeners. Pay attention to your hairstyle.
- Wear a layered outfit. Room temperature can change and so can your body temperature.
- Dress to impress!

Step 5: Visual Aids

A couple years ago, I attended a two-day event that introduced the California English Language Arts and English Language Development (ELA/ELD) standards. All the presenters used a template with a design that took up 20 percent of the space. The speakers did not reduce the number of words per slide, but instead reduced the size of the graphs, text, and images included on each slide. The overwhelming majority of slides had at least five bullet points and lots of text. I estimate that in those two days I saw the California Department of Education logo 500 times, along with 1,500 bullet points. Unfortunately, I remember more about the poor structure of all the slides than I do about the content the slides were designed to present. This is a prime example of visual aid failure.

Choosing Visual Aids

We're on step 5 and you still haven't spoken a word. But don't worry, you are making progress toward creating a good talk. You have content that's well organized and specifically designed for your audience, and you look presentable. For many talks, you could stop here. However, you may need to do one more thing: Include visual aids.

Before we go any farther, a word of warning: Visual aids are often used for the wrong reasons. Some speakers use them to hide because aids take eyes off the speaker and remove some of the pressure from the audience's focus. Other speakers use them to provide prompts in case they forget what they were going to say. These may seem like good ideas, especially for the beginning speaker, but visual aids actually diminish many messages rather than enhance them.

Preparing a visual aid distracts us from preparing the talk. Speakers typically spend too much time creating their PowerPoint slides and not enough time thinking about the more important aspects of creating a meaningful speech. How many times have you been bored by a speaker even though you were being shown fun, colorful slides? Glitzy graphics only impress the audience if they're supporting a strong speech.

Visual aids can also distract the listeners because listeners tend to focus on the visual aid rather than the speaker. Have you ever tried to talk to someone while they were watching TV or reading? Do they listen well? Doubtful. So, why would you want to build an attention-diverter into your speech? On that note, why bother speaking at all if everything you say is on your slides? Just send out an email with the PowerPoint attached!

People can attend to only one thing well at any given moment, and most research suggests that there is not a depth of understanding when attention is divided. When you include visual aids, you're asking listeners to give partial attention to you and partial attention to your visual aid. As they read the slide or listen to your musical background, they are not listening as well as they could to your words. *You* should be more important than your materials.

Of course, some talks require visual aids and some are better with visual aids. For example, at a training session about designing instruction, you can use slides to show examples of poorly created materials and improved materials to explain how to create better instructional programs. At the employee orientation, it may be helpful to have slides showing the correct way to fill out employment forms. A slideshow of the couple can be an adorable part of the rehearsal dinner or wedding reception: Here they are when they were both babies, at age six, at age 12; in scout uniform and soccer uniform; at high school graduation; on an early date; and so on.

Creating Visual Aids

I believe that the aids we normally see are quite poor. So, once you decide to include them in your presentation, how do you make visual aids better? This discussion will focus on PowerPoint, because it is still the most commonly used tool for presentations. However, the principles we're discussing still apply if you use Prezi, Keynote, Haiku Deck, or something else. If you use screen casting software, apply these principles to the screen you are capturing.

Is It On Point?

Your visual aid should be based on the purpose of the talk. Does it directly reflect the message? Is it completely on point? I once watched a speaker who included random cartoons in his PowerPoint because he wanted to break up the monotony. He thought they were funny, but they had no connection to his topic! Yes, there were some chuckles, but most of us thought, "I don't want to spend my time looking at cartoons right now!" They did not enhance the talk in any way; they simply derailed our train of thought and slowed down the presentation.

If you show something, it needs to be relevant. I will suggest later using images on your slides, but don't put up images that have nothing to do with your topic. Using pictures from your Hawaii vacation as a slide background is distracting; choosing a slide design from PowerPoint "just because I like it" is not ideal. Your audience will be left trying to find the connection— why did you choose the vintage background if your presentation is all about the future? Everything we see should be relevant to your message.

Is It Necessary?

Visual aids need to be absolutely necessary to help viewers understand the message. Think of the visual aids you typically see. They simply repeat what the speaker is saying, right? We are so used to seeing bullet points with complete sentences that it seems almost like heresy to say that this practice is not acceptable. Yes, someone will say that seeing the words reinforces hearing the words. I disagree. In his book *Multimedia Learning,* Richard Mayer (127) says showing "on screen text that is identical to the narration tends to hurt . . . understanding." He points out that everyone has a limited capacity for receiving information. If we are trying to read while listening, we will take in less information than if we were just reading or just listening. Rather than including every word of your talk in your slide deck, include only keywords that highlight the message. Look at the difference between the two slides in Figure 5-1. Which would you prefer? Which is more memorable for the audience? The slide on the right. When designing your slides, display only the most important information. Cut the extraneous words.

Figure 5-1. Bullets vs. Key Terms

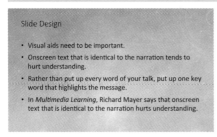

If a visual clarifies something we cannot easily follow verbally, that qualifies as important. Explaining how to swing a baseball bat, for example, will be more effective if you include visuals of proper stance, bat position, swing plane, and so on. Complex procedures may fit into this category as well.

Visual aids should be minimalistic and used sparingly. Is it critically important? Then use a visual aid. Otherwise, use your spoken words.

Are They Accessible?

Have you ever seen a visual aid and thought, "What the heck is that supposed to show?" Did it have little boxes with arrows from one to the next and labels you couldn't read or timelines with indecipherable dates and descriptions? What about a complex graph with tiny labels and criss-crossing lines? We have all been there.

Make sure your graphics and text are big enough, clear enough, vivid enough, and neat enough to be seen by everyone in the audience. Are the words and images right for the size of the room? Do the colors work? It is amazing how many speakers will say, "I know this is hard to see, but this picture shows. . . ." Why would you create a slide you know you have to apologize for? Visual aids should help the listeners, not make them reach for their glasses.

Visual aids also need to be accessible in another sense: They must be tailored to your audience's level. You would use different visuals for a room full of sixth graders than you would for a group of scientists when discussing some scientific principle. Use your audience analysis. Slides with jargon, technical terms, and complex diagrams will cause most listeners' eyes to glaze over and attention to wane. Step back and look at your projected visuals from across the room. For digital content, view it on the same sized screen as your audience will. Can you immediately grasp the content? If not, make it more accessible.

Do You Offer Variety?

In addition to the problem of slides filled with densely packed type, multiple bullet points, and complex flowcharts with arrows everywhere, there is another problem. Have you ever seen a visual aid and thought, "Isn't this the same slide I just saw?" I mentioned my experience at the ELA/ELD presentations in California at the beginning of this chapter. You can see why I had that thought if you look at Figure 5-2, which includes a few of the slides I saw that day.

When you're practicing, scroll through your presentation quickly. Do all the slides start to look the same? If the answer is yes, change them. Break the mold. Avoid bullet points entirely. Give your audience variety.

Figure 5-2. ELA/ELD Presentation

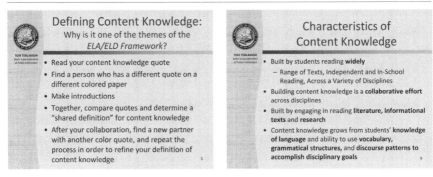

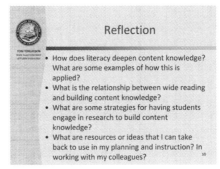

Are Your Visuals Simple?

Don't decorate your slides, design them. Presentation software makes it easy to put fun backgrounds and rainbow-colored letters with shadows on your slides. I used to use the slide on the left in Figure 5-3 in my talks. It's fun, isn't it? But is it good? How does it compare with the one on the right? I switched to the one on the right because I wanted my audiences to get my point, rather than get into discussions about the artistic merits of my slide. Remember, fancy backgrounds and odd fonts can be distracting. Don't be tempted by the gimmicks!

When you start to build your presentation, use the KISS principle. While there are a few different versions about what this acronym stands for, the most common one is "Keep It Simple, Stupid." That seems a bit harsh, so let's say it means "Keep It Simple, Speaker." If you have to share a lot of information, send an email or provide a handout so the audience can read all the material later. That's faster. (Most people read about 250 words per minute, but most speakers say about 150 words per minute.) If you can't make a simple visual aid, don't make a visual aid at all. Slides should merely reinforce what you're saying; they should not try to explain anything.

Figure 5-3. A Decorated and Simple Slide

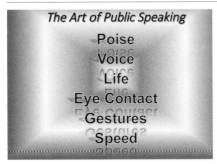

Don't create the kind of slides we always see. You are there to speak, and the audience wants to hear you, not struggle to interpret your visual aids.

Do Your Aids Use Images?

Look at the slides in Figure 5-4. Which would you prefer to see in a talk? I'm guessing it's the one on the right. Why, then, do so many presenters make the mistake of using word-dense, bulleted slides?

Figure 5-4. Text-Based vs. Image-Based Slides

RESOURCES

- Our company provides resources and tools for our customers providing several options for managing and completing the tasks required to keep their clients up to date.
- Our company has a group of trainers that can identify areas needing professional development and design and deliver instruction about topics that will be essential for successful implementation of our materials.
- Our company has a professional learning group that is designing and maintaining a digital library with professional development plans, curricular materials, and other resources making it possible for our customers to maintain state of the art techniques.

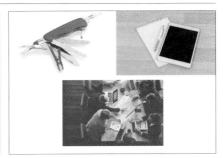

If you can, replace words with images. Think of the television commercials you see for animal rights organizations. They show picture after picture of sad dogs, uncared-for cats, and caged animals as a voice asks you to contribute a small amount of money each month to help. These commercials are very effective. A slide with bullet points telling us how many animals are mistreated, abandoned, or put to sleep is probably more informative, but will have less impact. Use only words on some slides, combine images and words on some slides, and use only images on others. Try making slides with no more than six words or three images, or one image plus six words. You won't always hit those targets, but they are targets worth aiming for.

When you use images, be aware that there is no law that says pictures must be small and placed on the side of the slide. When appropriate, make the image fill the screen and add key words on top (Figure 5-5).

Figure 5-5. Full-Screen Image

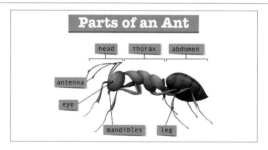

And one more point about images: They can change the meaning of words. Use that to your advantage when creating visuals for your presentation. For example, take a look at the two images in Figure 5-6. They may say the same thing, but they make you feel very different.

Think about images as advertisers do. Harness their power for your talk.

Figure 5-6. The Power of Visuals

We got a 6% raise

We got a 6% raise

Do Your Aids Use Audio?

Although I use the word *visual,* many aids now include an audio or audiovisual component. Start thinking about your presentation in terms of multimedia. For example, remember the pet-rescue commercial? There was a sad song playing in the background designed to emphasize the sadness of the words being spoken, right? How can you use music before, during, or after your talk to contribute to the mood you want to convey? What music can you play in the conference room as attendees walk in or out? What music should accompany the rehearsal dinner slideshow? What about a eulogy? These decisions should be considered carefully.

Finally, it is worth noting that someone else has probably already done a presentation on your topic. This means that you don't have to do all the talking! Search online for videos of experts talking about your topic and share them with your audience. Don't just tell the audience how something works; show them a video of it working.

If you can't find anything online, grab your computer, tablet, or smartphone and record yourself working with the equipment or doing the activity. Then bring that video to the training session. Your credibility will go up, and trainees will be able to see how to apply the instruction to the workplace. For a social event, like a retirement party, you could bring in video of people who could not attend but still wanted to offer best wishes. A multimedia experience is easy to create and certainly more appropriate for today's audiences.

Displaying the Visual Aid

A visual aid should not be revealed until the precise moment you want the audience to focus on it. If you reveal the aid before you start speaking about it, the audience will get distracted, wondering when you're going to explain the picture, or what you are going to do with it. Similarly, as soon as you are finished with the aid, remove it from sight. If not, the audience will continue to focus on it and not you, and start having side conversations discussing the picture's artistic merits. This comes from an understanding that constant visual stimulation is not necessary or advisable. PowerPoint has some simple, built-in commands that you can use to hide your presentation: Command + B turns the screen black and Command + W turns it white. If you are giving a PowerPoint presentation, use those commands. If you are using other visual aids or programs, make sure you have your own Command + B so you can keep your visual aids out of sight when you aren't using them. Keep the focus on you!

Key Points

- Don't assume that you need visual aids. They take attention away from you and can cause distraction.
- Make sure the visual aid fits the purpose of the speech and that it has a specific purpose.
- Does the visual aid contain something important? Don't simply display the text you are going to read to your audience; use key words and pictures to highlight important concepts.
- Check to ensure the visual aid is at the audience level. Will everyone understand what the slide means?
- Can every audience member see the aid? Think about the medium being used—what works on a large screen at the front of the room may not work on a computer screen.
- Avoid complex visuals—KISS.

- Use full-screen images, add appropriate sound, and include video when it makes sense.
- Reveal visual aids only when needed, and remove them immediately when finished.

Part 1 Postscript

VOCAL Preparation

Look back at the introduction to part 1. I promised to focus on creating a talk—the things you do *before* you open your mouth. I said that we create the message before we speak it, no matter the situation or whether the talk is for one person or many, in-person or digital delivery, or work or pleasure. I suggested paying attention to rule 1: Never speak unless you have something worth saying.

As I've mentioned, acronyms can be very powerful learning tools. Think of the five steps of building a talk as VOCAL preparation. Although the letters are not in the order in which you will prepare, it's still a useful mnemonic device to help you remember what to do to be ready to talk: Audience is always the first consideration; Content will determine the Organization and Visuals you create; and Looks is the last thing to consider. Whether you use the acronym or not, if you can check off each letter, you are ready to speak. You have analyzed your listeners, created a valuable message, put that into a powerful framework, enhanced your words, and addressed the way you look.

Use the following checklist to evaluate your talks:

Audience

- ☐ If I were listening to this talk, I would be interested and engaged.

Content

- ☐ Important: I only said things that matter.
- ☐ Connectors: I included things to make the audience think, "I get it! That connects to my life!"
- ☐ Explanations: I explained things that the audience would not have understood.
- ☐ Verbal viruses: I never said things such as "like" or "OK?" or "ya know."

Organization

- ☐ Grabber opening: After a few words, everyone in the audience was paying attention and curious to know more.
- ☐ Signposts: I had specific verbal markers to guide the listeners.
- ☐ Great closing: I didn't just stop talking. I had a powerful finish to my talk.

Looks

- ☐ I looked good. I dressed appropriately for the occasion.

Visual aids

- ☐ Easy to see: I made something large enough to be visible by everyone.
- ☐ Important: I only showed things that were critical to help my audience. I had very few words on the visual aid.
- ☐ Not decorated: I didn't have lots of extraneous decoration. I used images well.
- ☐ I incorporated multimedia when appropriate.

Part 2

As You Speak

Think about a time when you watched a speaker and thought, "Wow, he is good!" or "She was fantastic!" What was it that impressed you? Excellent grammar? Brilliant metaphors and similes? Seamless transitions? Terrific sentence structure? I'm guessing it was none of those. I bet it was something about the way the speaker delivered the message.

When we say, "That person speaks well," we don't usually mean, "That person *creates* good talks." While the *message* of a speech may, in fact, be great, what usually stands out in our minds is how that message is *presented*. Indeed, the way a speech is performed is more important than how it is built. That may seem surprising and perhaps even disappointing, but it's true. If you cannot deliver your talk well, no one will notice how well it was written. I disagree with the cliché that knowledge is power. I would argue that *communicating* knowledge is power. Excellent speakers do some things as they speak that make even ordinary or weak messages seem impressive. Similarly, the most brilliant ideas can seem worthless if poorly presented.

Speaking Is More Than Delivery

I realize that most people use the word *deliver* when discussing speeches, but I prefer the word *performance*. Delivery is easy: Hand someone a letter, drop off a package, say these words. But just saying words is not sufficient. Making an impact is a bit more difficult. You need to think of every talk as a performance. When you stand in front of trainees, you must do more than talk at them—you have to impress them. That requires performing. When you speak to the board, you want your idea to sound great. Don't say it, perform it. When you take the microphone at the retirement dinner, you want the audience to enjoy your words. How do you best entertain? By performing. When I gave my 16-year-old daughter the car keys for the first time, I spent a while thinking of what I wanted to say. Even though it was an audience of one, I wanted my words to have power. That means I had to perform, too.

I can imagine some readers' responses: This is just a training room, not a stage! That was just a conversation in the garage, not a movie set! I am not a performer! But know this: You *can* perform, and you will be more effective if you shift your thinking. Your words will have much more power if you begin to think like a performer.

The Fear of Public Speaking

I once attended a session given by Barbara McAfee at an ATD conference titled Unleash the Power of Your Full Voice. The session was all about adding life to your voice, which is an element of performance introduced in this part of the book. What struck me most about that session was the large number of attendees. I admit that I eavesdropped a bit on the conversations of those around me, and it was clear that most of them did not feel comfortable as speakers. I heard people say, "I never had any training about this" and "I'm afraid of being taped" and "I think my voice is too high."

We have all heard that people fear public speaking. For most, it is the performance that they fear, not creating the speech. And, now that you know that speaking is not simply delivering words, you may have even more trepidation. We dread having to get up in front of a group, whether that group is the staff at the monthly meeting, the guests at the party, or another group (large or small).

I believe this fear is overstated, but the widespread belief in this fear and the belief that getting up in front of a crowd is really difficult works to your advantage. It makes audiences forgiving—they're more likely to ignore some small flub, because they empathize. They know how it feels to be in your shoes, so relax a little bit and know the audience is behind you.

The question is, where does the fear come from? Remember the talk I gave to a group of farmers in western Kansas? After the talk, one audience member asked me if I wanted to see his farm. I realized that I needed to know more about farming and farmers if I wanted to be able to successfully communicate with them, so I said yes. What is the best way to see a large farm? From the air. We got into his two-seat, single-propeller plane, and soon began bouncing down the runway (which was just a dirt strip between his wheat fields). When we were airborne, I had a scary thought: What if something happened to him while he was flying the plane? I panicked. Why? Because I have no idea how to fly a plane. If I had known how to fly (and land!) a plane, I wouldn't have experienced that moment of fear.

I believe the fear of public speaking is also the result of a lack of knowledge. It is likely that no one ever gave you meaningful lessons about how to be well spoken. Once you learn how to perform a talk, I bet your fear of speaking will diminish.

Rule 2: Never let a poor performance diminish a good message.

Speaking effectively does not require skills that only a few can master. You don't have to become a new person, either—people can be effective with different styles. Use the six steps of performing talks that you'll learn in this section to help you adjust your style, and before you know it, you'll become an effective speaker. Your words are worth saying, so let's say them well.

Step 6: Poise

When I was in law school, I had a professor who wasn't a great speaker. He didn't have a problem getting words out, but he did something that made it difficult to pay attention to what he was saying—he fidgeted with his keys. Have you ever tried to listen to someone who continually jangled keys in their pants pockets? That term, we focused on those keys, not his words. When he stopped jingling his keys, we wondered when he would start again. When he started, we counted the seconds until he would stop. He may have been a terrific legal scholar with plenty of knowledge about property law to impart, but that was completely lost on us. One annoying habit ruined his lectures.

Common Problems

The first piece of effective performance is to develop poise. Dictionary definitions of poise include phrases such as *self-confident manner* and *composure*. While many speakers, especially those in new situations, do not feel calm, self-confident, or composed, you need to keep your unease from showing by controlling any odd nervous tics. Audiences forgive nerves that cause a slight quiver in your voice, but they will be less sympathetic to repeated, annoying tics because they make it difficult to pay attention to your words. Think of things that nervous speakers do. Have you seen speakers who tug at or squish their fingers? Have you seen speakers who constantly fidget with eyeglasses, pushing them up the bridge of their nose even if they're not slipping? What about speakers with happy feet or dance steps? One foot comes forward with heel down and toes up; that foot comes back and then the other foot comes forward. What about speakers who always twirl their hair or tuck it behind their ear? How about fidgeting with paper clips or pens, rolling and unrolling notes, rocking side to side, constantly adjusting papers, tugging at a collar, or repeatedly touching their nose? I'm sure you can add to this list. Over the next couple weeks, pay close attention to speakers and look for odd mannerisms. This activity will give you lots of ideas about behaviors to avoid.

I mentioned my law professor jangling keys in his pocket. He probably wasn't nervous because he had taught for years and given many lectures. It probably started as a nervous tic, and then somehow became a habit. Similarly, the principal at my children's high school always plays with the height-adjustment ring on the microphone stand. He never raises or lowers the mic, he simply tightens and loosens the ring that would make that possible as he holds the microphone. He isn't nervous, but he also isn't aware of this habit.

Speakers often do strange things and yet have no idea they are doing them. My son-in-law tells the story of a training session he went to in which one of the speakers had a very odd way of wearing his reading glasses. When he wasn't using them, he had them hang from his temples and swing below his chin. My son-in-law remembers watching the glasses swing, remembers that the glasses were tortoise shell, and remembers the speaker's name. He does not remember what the training session was about.

It is easy to get help. One option is to ask your staff if you do anything odd as you speak. If it makes you uncomfortable to ask others, set up your laptop or smartphone and record yourself in action. The good news is that most people have only one tic. It is rare to find someone who jangles coins and fidgets with the microphone stand, or tugs their fingers and plays with their hair. Once you are aware of the behavior, you will start to catch yourself as you do it. If you begin making a conscious effort to stop, over time, you will do it less and less.

Addressing Mistakes

What should you do when you make a mistake? Notice that I didn't say *if* you make a mistake. You will make mistakes. We say one word when we meant to say another, we have a little catch in our voice, we temporarily forget what we were going to say, we drop our notes, our slides don't advance, the website doesn't open—things happen.

There's no need to panic; audiences don't demand perfection, so you don't need to get flustered. Simply acknowledge the error:

> *I'm sorry. I meant to say . . .*

> *Oops, that was silly. Let's keep moving. . . .*

> *I lost my place. Bear with me, please.*

> *While we find someone to adjust the projector, I'll just tell you what is on the slide you should be seeing. . . .*

Poise includes handling glitches and flubs well. Recently, I gave a talk in Baltimore to a full auditorium. Unfortunately, there were a couple issues: The people in the control booth could not get my PowerPoint slides to appear, and then the batteries in my microphone died. Inside, I was thinking "Disaster!" and as I got more nervous, my body temperature started to rise. I did not feel calm and comfortable, but I faked calm and comfortable. And I was honest with the audience about the situation:

> *Ever have one of those days? This may be one for me. While they try to get things straightened out in the control booth and search for replacement batteries, I'm going to ask for your indulgence as I continue. I'll speak as loudly as I can, and I believe we'll be fine. Pretend you are looking at a screen with the letters PVLEGS on it . . .*

It's normal to become a bit flustered by an uncomfortable situation, but don't let it upset you. As I said, I get warm—although the temperature in the room didn't change, I felt like it had increased by 10 degrees. Some people get flushed faces. For others, their hands begin to sweat or their mouths may feel dry. Unfortunately, these aren't tics that can be controlled. You know what's happening, but if you stay calm, audiences won't pick up on those types of reactions. Act cool. Take a drink of water. You will settle down.

Strategies for Staying Poised

Remember how scared you felt the first time you got behind the wheel of a car? Going 25 miles an hour seemed dangerously fast. Now, driving is not remotely scary. Similarly, the more often you speak, the less fearful you will be, but some nervousness will always remain. I'm sure that my heart rate goes up before talks even though I have given hundreds of them. Of course, pointing out that experience will make being poised easier doesn't help you with the talks you are giving while gaining that experience. What can you do now to help you become calm and confident?

Find a Home Position

When I was on the debate team in high school and college, I had a certain place where I felt absolutely calm and confident. I would start behind the podium, but as I spoke, I would move to the side of the podium, put my elbow on the podium, and cross my feet. The look was relaxed yet powerful. If you watch me speak now, I still gravitate to that "home" position whenever I can. If there is no podium, I'll use the table next to me. At some point, I'll put my hand on the table, lean on it, and cross my feet. From that position, I feel comfortable and I know I am not doing anything to distract the listeners. However, I don't stay in that position. It is where I start, and it is a place I return to from time to time. Just like home.

Find your home position; it is different for everyone. If you are speaking while standing, do you want to have your left foot in front of your right? Both feet shoulder-width apart? One hand in your pocket? You aren't locked into whatever position you choose. You are simply finding a place to start, one where you feel comfortable.

Watch good speakers. How do they stand? Where do they put their hands? Where do their hands go after gesturing? Where do they go after they move around the stage? If you are speaking while seated, find a home position there as well. Do you want both feet on the ground, with your hands folded on the table? Left leg over the right? One hand on the table and one on the arm of the chair?

You've probably heard about power poses. Many body language books and speaking experts suggest certain postures for conveying power or calm, but if trying to adopt someone else's idea of how to stand and sit makes you uncomfortable, don't do it. The goal is to be more comfortable, not worried about how you are sitting or standing. What works for you?

It's important to note that being calm and confident does not mean being super relaxed. You may think that slouching in your chair at an interview conveys that you are laid back, calm, and confident. But it may also convey a lack of interest or disrespect. Let's think back to audience analysis for a minute. Will the interviewer interpret slouching the same way you do? Probably not. So, make sure your home position is where you feel calm, confident, and impressive. When I leaned against the podium at debate tournaments, I didn't seem less impressive than a speaker standing behind the podium. Knowing that your home position makes you seem impressive will also help you feel more calm and confident!

Be Prepared

The best way to stay poised is to be prepared. I feel better when I know that my talk is spot on. I don't practice until I get it right; I practice until I can't get it wrong. I feel more confident when I know I won't make avoidable mistakes. If you have done all you can possibly do to get yourself ready, you will be calmer and more confident when it is time to speak.

Surprises can be upsetting, and something out of the ordinary can take you off your game. The solution? Make sure there are no surprises! Visit the room where your training session will be; arrive early to test all the equipment; store backups of your presentation on a flash drive or in the cloud; and bring laptop chargers and spare batteries for your clicker. Your manager should find out who will be at the meeting so you aren't surprised if the regional manager decides to attend. Make sure you print materials well in advance instead of racing to the copy room minutes before the meeting. For the an event with more than one speaker, find out who else is speaking and in what order.

Try to predict audience responses, because an unexpected reaction can throw you off. Will someone in a training session be disappointed because she doesn't want to be there? Will there be upset employees when the reorganization is announced? Will there be interruptions for laughs at the toast?

Predict your responses, too. Most speakers are a bit nervous at the beginning but calm down once they get going. Expect that. Other responses can be predicted, too. For instance, I knew I would get choked up when I spoke at my son's wedding, so I prepared for it. If you know what's going to happen, your train of thought won't derail when it does.

Be prepared for physical changes, too. You will get thirsty, so bring some water. Check the temperature of the room, and know that it may be too warm or too cold, or that you may begin to warm up once you get going. Remember the tip in chapter 4? Layered clothing is a good idea.

Calm Your Nerves

Once you know your home position and have prepared for the unexpected, you're almost ready. Now you just have to figure out how to deal with the stress of actually giving your talk! If nerves are a big issue for you, look for resources that go in depth into calming behaviors and see what works for you. There are many methods to help people deal with stress. Some people meditate like a Zen master—breathe in for a count of four, then breathe out for a count of eight, and repeat 10 times. Others stand like Superman before their talk to feel powerful, or visualize the audience sitting in their underwear. Others engage in positive self-talk: "I can do this! I am ready!"

Here is what I find helpful:

Well before a talk, I visualize success. I create a mental picture of how I think the training session, meeting, keynote, or lecture would look if I do my job well. I also visualize what could go wrong. This helps me realize that the stakes are not all that high. I'm not alone in that single propeller plane where a mistake is fatal. Even if I make what I think is a catastrophic blunder, I'll survive and so will the listeners.

A few minutes before a talk, I find a way to be alone for five minutes. I make an excuse to leave the fray: "I'm just going to get a drink/go to the bathroom/make sure I reply to this text I just got." I spend the time quietly. I don't mentally rehearse, but rather let my mind do what it wants.

When it is time to talk, I take my time to get myself ready: I walk up slowly, place my notes on the podium or table, pick up the clicker, or adjust the microphone. Then I find my home position. Not rushing into the talk gives the audience time to settle into attention, and it gives me time to settle my nerves.

During the talk, I monitor my comfort level. No one will get upset if you pause for a drink or take off your jacket or sweater. Take your time. And I don't allow physical distractions (Am I going to cough? Am I sweating too much?) to bother me.

Key Points

- Discover your nervous tic or your annoying habit. Work on eliminating those distractions.
- Don't panic. Mistakes are inevitable. Calmly acknowledge them and move on.
- Find your home position for various speaking situations (at the podium, standing alone, seated at a conference table, seated without a desk or table). Start speaking from a place where you feel comfortable, and then return to it whenever you need to.
- The best defense is a good offense. Prepare for all possibilities. Eliminate the element of surprise. Learn everything you can about the venue. Practice. Practice. And then practice again.
- Use relaxation strategies. Take deep, calming breaths. Visualize success. Engage in positive self-talk. Move slowly.

Step 7: Voice

There was a person in my University of Colorado state teaching certification program who was very soft-spoken. During the program, we often had to develop mock lessons and test them out on our classmates to simulate school situations. His lessons were inaudible. No matter how often we told him we couldn't hear, he seemed incapable of speaking louder. I remember thinking that if he ever got into a classroom, it would be a disaster. Kids don't have the inclination or patience to struggle to hear things. You may be thinking that adults don't either.

It's Not Just About Being Loud

Listeners need to hear every word you speak. Your audience should never say or think, "What did he say?" or "I didn't catch her last point." Different books and experts vary the language—*volume, enunciation, articulation, elocution, projection*—but I prefer the word *voice* to simplify thinking. If you pay attention to how your voice sounds, you'll be fine.

Have you ever had a teacher, or perhaps several teachers, who told you to "speak up"? As children, some of us were timid, so we answered quietly. Whether you were in front of the class illustrating how to solve an equation or answering a question during a class discussion, your teacher may have said, "We can't hear you!" "Project!" "Speak loudly!" "Volume!" Some of that advice was incorrect: If you speak loudly, people will not enjoy listening to you. It is also likely that those admonitions helped reinforce your fear of speaking—I tried but I got criticized! This lack of self-confidence led to you being even more timid and quiet.

That lack of confidence has continued into adulthood for many people. You may be one who never speaks up in meetings, not because you have no ideas but because you are soft-spoken and feel intimidated by louder co-workers. You don't have to compete with big voices. The only thing you must do is make sure everyone can hear every word. Don't speak loudly; speak loud enough. Indeed, a soft voice can be powerful. When my father said, "Erik, come here" very quietly, I knew I was in big trouble.

Your job is to make sure your voice is loud enough for the space. If the room is large, your voice should be loud enough that everyone in the audience can comfortably hear you. If you're using a microphone, adjust your volume level so that everyone in the audience can hear you without being blown away.

Change Volume Levels

Effective speakers change volume levels when they talk. They don't speak too softly to be heard or too loudly to damage eardrums, but they do emphasize key points with varying decibels:

> *[Quietly] Let's be very serious for a moment. We need a 99 rating or higher when we are audited on sterilization. Ninety-nine. [A little louder] If anyone . . . ANYONE . . . fails to follow these procedures, it will be cause for immediate termination.*

> *[Quietly] We were sneaking up from the back. They had no idea we were there. We got very close and [Loudly] SLAMMED THE DOOR SHUT! [Normally] They must have jumped five feet!*

Small changes can have a big impact.

Make Sure They Hear Every Word

Years ago, I had ham for dinner at a friend's house in Georgia. When I asked how the ham was prepared, the host said, "I pore coecola over the hayam."

I'm from Michigan, and had never heard of coecola, so I said, "I'm sorry, but I didn't catch that. Can you repeat that?"

"Coecola?"

"Yes, what is coecola?"

After a couple minutes, she brought out a bottle of Coca-Cola. Just your basic Coke. A great marinade for ham as it turns out, but a hard word to decipher if you don't know the vocal pattern of the region. Comedian Jeff Foxworthy has a bit about this issue. He jokes about the word *widjadidja*: "Hey, you didn't bring your truck widjadidja?" That may be closer to what most of us say instead of "with you, did you," but it humorously points out a problem. You must make sure your voice clearly delivers every word in a way your audience understands.

The problem may be related to dialect, but there's often another cause. You may hear speech coaches talk about articulation, enunciation, or elocution, which is just another way of saying to make sure every word is heard. Volume isn't the problem these words address; mumbling or blurring words together is. "Yuno-whutumsayin?" may work in the dugout, but "Do you know what I'm saying?" will be preferred in many other places.

Don't be lazy. Speak each word clearly.

Odd Vocal Patterns

Paying attention to your voice means paying attention to your voice's patterns. Some people's words fade away at the end of a sentence.

> *This is a problem. Many people do not finish their sentences. They start out well, but then get progressively quieter.*

Every word must be heard, not just the first few.

The opposite happens, too. Sometimes voices go *up* at the end of a sentence, as if every statement is a question. Have you heard speakers who do that?

"I went to the store? There was a sale? I bought this jacket?"

Are you telling me or asking me? If you say, "That is annoying" the same way you say, "Is that annoying?" you will annoy your listeners.

Be Pleasant to Listen to

Have you been in a restaurant or a similar place and heard a laugh across the room that made you cringe? Most laughs make listeners smile or laugh even without knowing what they are laughing at, but occasionally you've probably heard a laugh that made you hope no one at the table knew any more amusing stories.

Unfortunately, some voices are cringe-worthy as well. Can you think of a comedian or television or film character who has intentionally created such a voice? They're modeled after voices we have all run into at some point. I once overheard someone telling a story at the gym—his harsh, jarring way of talking stood out even in a room full of noises and conversations.

We are used to our voices, so it is difficult to be objective. Some of you may be hyper-critical, thinking that you sound funny on recordings and worrying about things that don't matter ("I think my voice is too high"). Fortunately, the odds are excellent that your voice sounds fine. But you need to be sure and to know how others hear you. Record yourself. Be brutally honest. Ask trusted friends: "Is it tiring to listen to me?" "Do I sound strident/raspy/rough?" "Am I the voice of the reasonable person on the sitcom or the voice of the crazy friend?"

If vocal communication is important to your success, take corrective steps. Record yourself, listen, and re-record with the goal of sounding better. Play with your voice: Try to emulate a jazz station DJ or the narrator on the nature channel. If necessary, work with a vocal coach. Improving the sound of your voice will bring benefits.

Key Points

- Make sure every word you say can be heard easily by everyone in your audience.
- Have a voice that is just right for the space: not too loud, not too soft. Adjust your volume during the talk to add interest and emphasize ideas.
- Pronounce words carefully. No listener should ever say, "I'm sorry, but I didn't catch that."
- Pay attention to how your voice sounds. Make sure to avoid odd vocal patterns such as making every sentence sound like a question or fading out at the end of sentences. Work on developing a pleasant-sounding voice.

Step 8: Life

I once visited the Ebenezer Baptist Church, a National Historic Site, in Atlanta. It's the church where Martin Luther King Jr. was baptized and where he was a pastor. His funeral was held there. I sat in one of the pews and listened to recordings of his sermons. As I listened, I remembered why, upon hearing him speak when I was young, I chose to use him as the model of what a speaker should be. Yes, his messages were excellent, but I have never heard anyone else with King's ability to inspire listeners. The passion in his voice was contagious. My goal has always been to have that kind of passion when I speak.

The Most Important Element

Flat. Monotonous. Boring. Dull. Sleep-inducing. Unexciting. Unfortunately, these and similar words describe many of the talks we hear in the workplace and our personal lives. By far the biggest growth area for all speakers is adding more life to their voice. Books on speaking typically mention *inflection, vocal modulation, pitch, expression,* and *enthusiasm,* but I think these are unclear and inaccurate descriptors. *Pitch* sounds like something a choir director would care about, and *enthusiasm* is inappropriate if you are talking about how many injuries occurred on the loading dock last year. If you create a wonderful message that does require enthusiasm, but present it without that emotion, your audience will have little enthusiasm about the topic. Let's simplify the discussion by using one simple term: *life*. Add life to your talks and listeners will hear feeling, emotion, and passion.

In the introduction to part 2, I asked you to recall the great speeches you've heard and remember what made them memorable. More often than not, I bet you thought of the emotion conveyed by the speaker's voice. Yes, an idea can be so powerful that it makes listening enjoyable, but we usually respond best to passionate speakers who add life to their words. They make us care about those words and make us feel the way they feel.

Let's explore a bit more about how important life is to speaking. Think about how you hear these phrases in your head:

That was the greatest game I have ever seen!

I loved that dog, and putting her down was the hardest thing ever.

Son, if you ever get behind the wheel drunk, you will never drive this car again.

So there I am in my underwear trying to dry my pants over the campfire, when the seat of my pants catches fire.

I bet you "heard" each of these a different way. The life used in one sentence wouldn't work in another. And an absence of life would diminish the words. The way you say words can even change their meaning.

Think about the sentence, "I think that is a great idea." How would you say it so that I believe you are excited about my idea? Can you think of a way to say the phrase that makes it seem as though you are the only one who likes my idea? Emphasizing the *I* in "*I* think that is a great idea" makes me finish the sentence with "but no one else does" in my head. Emphasizing *think* in "I *think* that is a great idea" makes me wonder if you have doubts about my idea because it implies "but I am not sure it is." And if you know someone who excels at being sarcastic, you know that those words can be said in a way that makes me think my idea is terrible. Play with short phrases that can be delivered in very different ways. For example, "I'm thinking we should go there" might mean "only I think that," or "I am not yet sure," or that "we should go instead of others," or that "we should go there instead of that other place." Change the meaning by changing your inflection to help you develop your expressive skills.

The way you say your words can make listeners feel what you want them to feel, and it can change the meaning of the words. Unfortunately, the way you say your words can also make people lose interest in them. That is how important life is—it is the most important feature of engaging speaking.

Imagine a 1 to 10 scale for rating life, in which 1 is "dreadfully boring monotone" and 10 is "tremendously lively and engaging." Mentally score every speaker you hear. You'll quickly notice that speakers with a score of 8 and above are rare and command more respect. Once you get a sense of how others rate, record and score yourself. Then start working to move up the scale.

I'm Not That Kind of Person

"But I'm not that kind of person. I'm not dynamic. I'm not a showman. I'm not exciting." What if you think of yourself as just a good, regular talker? That's fine, as long as good, regular talk leads to success in your workplace and social speaking occasions. However, for many people, who they are is not who they want to be. You are reading this book because you want to be a better speaker, right? Well, improving speaking requires continuous effort. It would be wonderful if you could read this book one time and say, "I've got it! I am a fantastic speaker! Put me in any speaking situation, and I will nail it!" Unfortunately, that is unlikely. Given that adding life is the most important thing you can do to be an impressive communicator, you'll need to put in some work to reach the next level. Stretch yourself. Raise the bar.

If you have a message you care about, listeners need to be able to hear that you care. That doesn't mean you have to be exuberant or excited or over-the-top. Speakers can convey passion in quiet ways. I have seen soft-spoken people convey deep concern for their topics, because something in the way they spoke let me know they had a strong belief in what they were saying.

Subtle changes in inflection count, too. Listeners will notice. But if listeners do not hear emotion, subtle or not, they will tune out. Where in your talk should you convey excitement? Anger? Sadness? Joy? Amusement? Disgust? Worry? Enthusiasm? If your talk does not include words designed to generate emotions, you have built a poor talk. Rewrite it. If your talk does have words that should make the audience react emotionally, work on adding life to those words.

What do you want to emphasize? Where do you want the audience to understand how serious something is, how funny something is, how tragic something is, and so on. Underline those words. Record yourself as you say them. Listen to the words and then record again with more and more feeling until you reach the level needed to make the words stand out.

Make the Life Match the Words

Not every sentence demands liveliness. Indeed, audiences are put off by speakers that seem too enthusiastic and too animated. Have you ever felt like telling a speaker to settle down? Listeners can detect when you're trying too hard. Have you been in a situation in which the right answer was wrong so you convincingly told a white lie? "No, I don't think anyone noticed your mistake. Don't worry about it." You probably added a bit of life to those words to make them believable. Did it work? Maybe. Most often, though, audiences know if you are faking emotion. Say, "This new procedure is great!" in a way that conveys enthusiasm, but only if you are truly enthusiastic about it. Be genuine.

Your goal is always to have the perfect blend of message and feeling, but if you are going to make a mistake, err on the side of adding extra feeling. That way, you guarantee that your audience is paying attention. No one expects a trainer to say, "The new credit card reader will not allow swiping the card, but will only allow inserting the card into the chip reader" as if that were the most amazing thing to ever occur. But no one expects a manager to say, "Kim is the employee of the month" in a way that indicates complete lack of interest, either. Do you know the joke about the new employee who finishes with the punch line, "That wasn't the copier!"

That was the shredder!!" Even if you don't, you can probably guess how it might go. Good readers "hear" lines being delivered in the appropriate way. Good speakers deliver those lines with the proper feeling.

Don't Use That Tone of Voice With Me!

When I was a teenager, my father would say, "Don't use that tone of voice with me!" when he detected a kind of life in my words that he didn't appreciate. I said, "Yes, Dad, I'm listening," but somehow those innocent words made him angry. If you have teenaged children, you can relate.

There is a cautionary note here for all speakers: Control unwanted inflection. Be aware of ways you add expression that can harm your message. Perhaps you think you are speaking in a matter-of-fact way, but your listeners hear an emotion or feeling they don't like. Was there a little disgust in the way you said that? Condescension? Dismissiveness? You want to make sure that you are in control of your tone of voice, adding feeling only when it helps the message. I might have been grounded less often if I had known this years ago.

Watch and Learn From Impressive Speakers

There is not one correct way to be lively. Watch other speakers, such as film and television stars, evangelists, motivational speakers, or politicians. Don't focus on their message or whether you agree with it. Just pay attention to how they add inflection, emotion, and passion to their words. They won't all have the same style, but they will have ways of engaging listeners with the feeling they add to their words.

I said earlier that you shouldn't mimic other speakers. But it can be a fun exercise to help you develop your own vocal variations. For example, I would mimic the way Martin Luther King Jr. finished the "I Have a Dream" speech to expand my expressiveness. And, perhaps oddly, I would also mimic the unexpressive way Eeyore or comedian Steven Wright speak to help me learn how to convey lack of emotion. I don't talk like any of them when I present, but I do reflect their influences. They have given me a range of emotions to draw upon to make my words more interesting.

Find speakers that you admire and speak along with them to learn how to expand your range, too.

◇◇

Key Points

- Adding life is the number one way to make any talk better. All speakers need more life in their voices.
- Avoid being dull. Audiences need to hear feeling, emotion, and passion.
- Stretch yourself. Do more than you think you can. Everyone can be more impressive.
- Add the appropriate expression. Don't try to make the unexciting exciting. Make sure your inflection matches your message.
- Practice. Raise the bar every time you speak. Progress slowly but steadily.

◇◇

Step 9: Eye Contact

Think of conversations you have with good friends. As you talk, you look at each other, right? Why? What goes through your head if your friend is looking somewhere else? My former business partner was always scanning the room when we went out to eat. Occasionally, he would say, "Isn't that [insert name of some local celebrity/sports figure]?" I got the message that our conversation was less important than attempting to spot someone famous. It was very annoying. Eye contact matters.

The Importance of Eye Contact

Have you ever felt as though someone was staring at you? You glance over and sure enough, a person is staring. How does that make you feel? A bit ill at ease? Self-conscious? Curious? Maybe all three? Have you ever had a conversation with someone who never broke eye contact? You probably thought you couldn't look away either, but I bet you really wanted that person to stop staring, right? Eye contact is powerful.

Audience members know when they are being looked at, and they feel acknowledged. Simply glancing their way is enough to show that you notice and value their presence. People who weren't looking at you start looking at you, and people who were looking at you will feel more connected. There is no substitute for direct eye contact, and it is crucial to engagement. Looking above the listeners' heads will not work. You and your audience may not see eye-to-eye on the issues, but you will see each other eye-to-eye.

Where Should You Look?

Some speakers are note-bound, reading at attendees from their notes or the projected slide, and seldom if ever looking at the audience. Most speakers have a habit of looking at only some people. Perhaps they think they only need to address the manager or supervisor instead of the other staff at the meeting. At a birthday dinner, people seated near the guest of honor often get a lot of attention, while large parts of the room are ignored. This may seem defensible. After all, the manager makes the decisions at the staff meetings, and the party is for the person turning 50. However, that does not mean that no one else matters. You always want to connect with everyone in attendance—you want the entire staff to be with you, and you want the entire audience to enjoy your stories. Look at them.

Those sitting in the middle of the room often get the most notice, because it's easy to look straight ahead, and turning your head to look left and right is not a natural movement. People who sit up front at the side might as well be invisible—no one looks there. This may be a good tip for those of you who want to know the best place to hide at conferences and required training sessions. However, I offer this information as a tip about how to avoid a mistake most speakers make. Think about where you look when you speak. Work toward fairness, looking at all listeners equally. Record yourself giving your talk and evaluate all the aspects of your performance, including where you look. Ask a trusted friend or co-worker to let you know if you missed paying attention to someone at the meeting or some section of the audience. During your talk, make a conscious effort to look to the sides of the room. Over time, you will get into the habit of making eye contact with every listener.

Learning From Looking

Audience members like to feel noticed and valued, but there is another reason to look at your listeners: They provide feedback. When I'm giving a talk, I don't need the session evaluation forms to know how well I did. My audience tells me all I need to know. For example, your talk is not going well if three people are checking email, two are yawning repeatedly, one is looking out the window, and four are sitting with their heads propped up by their hands. On the other hand, your talk is going well if everyone is watching you, everyone smiled at your joke, and faces were serious when you spoke about a serious topic.

Sometimes you can adjust on the spot. If you have a training break planned for 2:30 p.m., but the post-lunch doldrums seem to be kicking in at 1:55, move up break time. If you planned for 30 minute group discussions, but it looks as though 20 minutes was sufficient, call everyone back early. If you've covered everything in your talk, it's fine to end the meeting early. If you planned to tell the whole story about what happened in Las Vegas, but notice that some in the audience are looking worried that you might tell the part that was supposed to stay in Vegas, tell the abridged version. Watch people's expressions for clues that you need to modify your talk.

Sometimes you can't adjust on the fly. Maybe you built a presentation that you thought would be engaging, but when you present it you discover that it's falling flat. You can't rebuild it right now, but you can make changes for next time based on the audience response.

Often, you'll find that some people look interested and some don't. Notice that. Do those who are not interested have something in common? It's possible that your talk is unwittingly targeted at one type of listener. Again, make changes next time to reach every type of listener. A speaker should never be oblivious to the listeners' reactions. Look at each member of the audience and learn from them.

Cultural Differences

Eye contact is not universally desired. In some cultures, it is not expected or, possibly, not acceptable. In *Other People's Children,* Lisa Delpits speaks about the "culture of power." There is a culture of power in a society. You can debate whether that culture is good or bad, but her point is simple: No one should be locked out of that culture because they haven't been taught the skills needed to join. You don't have to change and your style is not "wrong," but *if* you want to make it in the culture of power, you must know how the game is played.

Know your audience. In American culture, the rules include eye contact. If you are not comfortable making eye contact because you have been raised in a culture that doesn't value it, you must work to overcome your discomfort.

Know Your Stuff

Perhaps the biggest barrier to eye contact is being insufficiently prepared. You can't look at your listeners if you are reading your notes. You can't visually engage your audience if you are facing the screen because you are using the projected slides as a cheat sheet. You should be so familiar with what you are going to say that you can say it without notes or prompts from the screen.

Recall my story about talking to a large group in a Baltimore auditorium. A technical difficulty prevented my slides from being projected from the control booth, and the schedule would not allow for taking time to figure out the problem. My slides are not full of text (see step 5: Visual Aids), but they aren't blank either. I use them to highlight and reinforce key concepts, but I don't use them as reminders for myself. I ended up giving the talk without my visual aids, but I know my presentation so well that in my head, I could see every slide. You see, not only do I not want visuals to distract the audience; I do not want visuals to distract me. I want to engage with the audience.

Are you worried that you might forget something? You've probably seen speakers who interrupt themselves: "Wait a minute. Let me find my place. Um, just a second. Just a second. Wait. Oh, here I am. The most important consideration in preparing for retirement is. . . ." It happens, so it is acceptable to have notes available. But just notes, not a full text. At some point in creating a talk, you should write down every word you are going to say because this is the best way to make sure your content is what it should be. However, to facilitate eye contact, you need to reduce your full text to a few key words. If you have full sentences in front of you, you will become a reader, not a speaker. With key words, simply look down when you get stuck, and let them mentally trigger, "Oh yes, I know what I was going to say." Then look at the listeners. Remember Uncle Bob's antics after eight margaritas? You don't need to have every word of that story in front of you. You were there. You remember it. That's why one or two trigger words will suffice. Look down—see Carlos and Charlie's—look up, and then tell the story. Your message may come out differently each time you tell it, but the essence will be there. If you prepared well, you may not even need to look at the key words, but it is always nice to have them.

Of course, you may need to write down more words for a technical talk because it is difficult to remember all the regulations in the act or the numbers in the financials. Listeners will forgive you for occasionally focusing on your notes, but they expect you to look at them the rest of the time.

Practice your talk, but don't memorize it. You don't need to deliver the exact words. For example, if you wrote, "The most important consideration in discussing building morale is. . . . " you may actually say, "The most important consideration in talking about building morale is. . . ." That's fine.

Key Points

- Every talk is a conversation magnified. Look directly at all the people you are addressing. Eye contact connects you with your listeners.
- Be aware of where you look. Make sure you don't miss some parts of the room or some people in your audience.

- Use eye contact to learn from your listeners. Pay attention to audience responses and use the responses as feedback. Adjust your talk based on what you see.
- Be aware of cultural differences, but know that in Western cultures, eye contact is crucial.
- Know your talk inside and out. You cannot make eye contact while reading your speech or checking your notes.

Step 10: Gestures

Remember how my wife, Anne, opens her talk about the Olympics? She has another unique feature: She has the most expressive hand motions. When she says, "There were cobblestones at the start of the ride," her hands demonstrate the bumpiness of the road. When she says, "It wasn't raining, but there was a bit of a mist as we rode," her hand motions somehow make it clear that there was something in the air around the riders. I like hearing about Anne's bike ride, but I am even more interested when I can "see" and "feel" her ride. It is impossible to look away as she speaks, and her stories come alive with her effective hand motions.

Do you know someone like Anne? Don't you love watching them as you listen? Great gestures improve every talk.

The Importance of Gestures

Gestures add interest, but they do more than that. In a written work, you'll see text changes that are designed to influence the way you read the words. I used some earlier: I think that is a great idea; I *think* that is a great idea. You read "Stop it" differently than you read "**STOP IT!**" Similarly, gestures can influence the way we hear words. "Let me tell you something" seems a bit more ominous if the speaker is wagging a finger in front of your face as he speaks. When added to a certain life in the voice, it can make you fear that something big is about to happen. Gestures emphasize key points. And let's add one more point about gestures. Imagine that I am trying to teach you how to hold a baseball bat. I can talk about knuckle alignment and distance from the knob of the bat, but it will sink in better if I use my hands to show you the proper way to hold a bat. Gestures demonstrate.

Hand Gestures

When I say to think of gestures, most readers will think of *hand* gestures. Think of some common hand gestures: You may hold up three fingers when you say, "Let's look at three key ideas." This is a way of visually underlining the words. "The dog was very little" may be said while holding your hands about a foot apart. This is a way of clarifying the words.

These are descriptive hand gestures because you use your hands to show the words. Descriptive gestures are the easiest to develop. Read the following story and think of places where you could use your hands to help the audience picture the words.

> *Our cats only go outside when we go outside. They behave like dogs, staying in the yard and coming in when called. One evening as we came in from eating on the patio, we called the cats, and they came bounding in. We didn't notice until she was inside that Cleo had a live mouse in her mouth. In hindsight, yelling, "Cleo, drop it!" was probably a bad idea, because now we had a mouse running around the dining room. For some reason, my wife got a broom and a dustpan; I got a small bucket. Madness ensued: The cats were skittering around the dining room batting at the mouse, my wife was poking at it with the broom and waving the dustpan around, and I was trying to drop the bucket on it every time it ran by me. After a few minutes, we cornered the mouse. Both cats were staring at it, Anne was holding the broom in the ready position, and I was sneaking up to it. I moved very slowly until the bucket was right over the mouse. Then, bam! I slammed down the bucket. Mouse captured.*

How would you use hand gestures to emphasize points of this story? Can you hold your hands like Anne's to show how she poked at the mouse? Can you hold your hands in a way that makes listeners visualize you holding a small bucket? Some talks have many opportunities for descriptive hand gestures.

Often, talks do not describe and there is no obvious opportunity for a gesture. In these instances, some speakers don't move their hands, resorting instead to clutching the sides of the podium, holding their notes, or hiding their hands in pockets. Good speakers, though, use emphatic hand gestures to emphasize their words. If you pound the table as you say, "I will not [slam fist on table] tolerate that behavior, young man!" your son will know how mad you are.

Fist pounding is, thankfully, not common in the workplace, but more subtle gestures are. Become sensitive to how and when speakers move their hands. At a meeting, I once caught myself holding my right hand six inches in front of my face with my index finger held out as if I were pointing at the ceiling while saying, "I'm wondering if there is another way to do this." Why that gesture? What does a little finger wag have to do with other ways of doing something? Nothing. The finger wag is about sustaining interest and somehow drawing more attention to the words. You may have a different way of gesturing if you say those words.

Must hands always be in motion? No, but strive to have more motion than not. Gesturing hands add impact to your talk. As an added benefit, if you are using your hands to gesture, you will not be using them to do some distracting fidgeting. However, be aware of repeating the same gesture over and over. I watched a commercial for a local car dealer that demonstrated the problem:

> We have the best deals! [hands held six inches apart and moving as if they were doing a small karate chop] No deal is refused. [small karate chop] We'll take any trade. [small karate chop] Nobody beats our prices. [small karate chop]

The gesture becomes the focus, not the words: "See? There it is again!" Comedians have a field day mimicking the signature gestures of famous people. Don't make the mistake of having a signature gesture. Good speakers have a range of hand motions to call upon.

Facial Gestures

People can convey a lot of emotion with their faces. You've probably asked someone "Is something wrong?" or "What are you so happy about?" simply based on his or her expression. Facial expressions can also negate words: If your friend says, "No, I feel fine," but her face says, "I feel terrible," you believed the face, didn't you? What we see on someone's face is a crucial component of communication. Good speakers know this and think about how to use their faces to complement their message. "I'm worried about the way you handled this" said with a furrowed brow indicates seriousness. "Are you serious?" said with eyebrows raised indicates amazement. "Sure, Dad" said with an eye roll indicates a teen about to be grounded.

Audiences will mimic your face. If you say, "Guess what?" with eyebrows raised and wide eyes, people in your audience will look back at you with raised eyebrows. I am not suggesting that you want to get into a game of Monkey See, Monkey Do, but rather that you can use facial gestures to prime listeners for your message.

Body Gestures

There are entire books about body language, but I don't want to go into that level of detail here. As I mentioned, standing like Superman may improve your confidence, while crossing your arms over your chest may indicate that you are not open to meeting people. People can read all sorts of things into the way you sit, but I prefer to think about body movements the same way we think about hand or facial movements: gestures that can add or detract from your words.

Think of how you might move your head and body as these words are spoken:

> He was supposed to aim at the piñata, but came at my head. I ducked just in time.

> As I presented my idea, the chairman folded his arms and turned away from me kind of like this, so I knew it wasn't going well.

People are more likely to freely use gestures of all types when speaking socially. However, it is a mistake to believe that workplace situations demand some sort of stiff, formal delivery. Fellow employees will appreciate well-told stories about customer interactions if they are accompanied with descriptive body gestures. Trainers should change body positions to help trainees see how to correctly lift items as they stock the shelves.

When I conduct workshops, I sit down when I want attendees to converse with me. Sitting down means that I am not the subject matter expert imparting knowledge, but rather a member of the group. When I stand back up, attendees know I am back in my SME role and about to share something new. Standing and sitting can be body gestures? Sure. Think of other ways you have seen speakers move their bodies as they talk. There is a difference between sitting back in a chair at a conference table and leaning in, right? If, as you talk, you put your elbows on the table and lean forward to ask, "Is there another way to accomplish the same goal?" you are drawing more attention to yourself and to your question. If you shrug your shoulders as you say, "I don't know, but I have some questions about this proposal," those body gestures will add some heft to your hesitation about the item under discussion.

Using All Three

Although I presented them separately, we don't use our gestures separately. I don't think, "I'll add a hand gesture here, a facial gesture there, and two body gestures here and here." Great storytellers have synchronized gestures that combine hand, face, and body motions for maximum impact. They shrug and raise their eyebrows to answer the question, "Did you like what you saw?" They tilt their head forward while furrowing their brow to say, "Did I hear that right?" Keeping your mouth open as you lean forward while holding your palms up helps to convey, "What did you just do?"

Watch others in the workplace. Who has an expressive face and active hand gestures? Just by watching them, which of your co-workers "says" a lot? If you are one of those people, great! You are fun to watch when you speak. If you aren't one of those for whom all gestures naturally flow, work to become more interesting to watch.

Did You Mean That?

Remember when we discussed tone of voice in step 8? Some speakers give unintended messages because they aren't aware that the life in their voice is conveying the wrong meaning to their words. Unintended gestures can create problems, too. Years ago, I worked for a woman who hated being challenged. A true micromanager, Jane ignored input from knowledgeable employees and instead told them what she wanted them to do. She knew enough to say the right words, which I assume is how she got promoted. Her gestures, though, revealed her actual thoughts. I remember asking, "Can I ask you a question about this?" Even though she said, "Yes," her pursed lips and slightly tilted head said, "Whatever, jerk. Go ahead, but I'm not interested." I seriously thought about handing her a mirror so I could say, "Do you know what you look like right now? Is that what you want to convey?" She left the company before I did, however, so the plan I was saving for my last day never happened.

Gestures are important. They can enhance words, but they can also undermine them. What messages do you give to people watching you? Make sure they match your desired intentions.

Key Points

- Gestures help the audience visualize your words. They engage listeners.
- Use a range of hand gestures for emphasis and for describing. Avoid using the same gesture over and over.
- Facial gestures matter. The expression on your face lets the audience see how you feel about your topic.
- Your body position is important. Gestures such as leaning in or shrugging add meaning to your words.

- Synchronicity is powerful. Matching hand, face, and body gestures with well-written words creates an impressive presentation.
- Be aware of unintended gestures. Make sure your face and body gestures do not undercut your message.

Step 11: Speed

Ben Stein is an author, speechwriter, political commentator, and lawyer. Many people know his name because of a bit part in the movie *Ferris Bueller's Day Off*. In that movie, he played a high school economics teacher whose delivery put the class into a stupor. One feature of the delivery was the deadly pace of the talk. His lesson about the Great Depression has become a cinema classic:

> *The House of Representatives, in an effort to alleviate the effects of the—anyone? anyone?—the Great Depression, passed the—anyone? anyone?—the tariff bill, the Hawley-Smoot Tariff Act, which—anyone? raised or lowered? raised—tariffs.*

Many years later, his rhythmic repetition of "anyone? anyone?" is still widely remembered.

Slow and steady may win the race, but slow and steady loses your audience. Why do people fall asleep on long train rides? Why do parents drive the car around the neighborhood with toddlers who aren't going to sleep? Constant rhythm acts like a hypnotic drug, lulling people to sleep. Some speakers have the same effect. Pay attention to the speed of your words.

Slow Down

"Speak slowly" is a common piece of advice. But why would someone suggest that if slow talkers can make listeners nod off? Because speakers often talk fast when they get nervous. A talk that may have been eight minutes when practiced at home becomes six minutes and 43 seconds when presented to the big audience. Nervousness makes us speak more quickly. If you find yourself racing, it's good advice to slow down.

Some speakers purposely speak too quickly. I was working with some trainers in Oakland as I was writing this book, and one of them said something very concerning: "I only have one hour and 50 minutes to cover all of this, so I am going to have to go at super speed."

This is not a good idea. I will talk more about this in the workplace training section, but racing through a presentation can be disastrous if you're trying to convey information. You can pretend that you "covered a topic," but don't be surprised when you discover that no one got it. Whether unintentional or intentional, presenting at a consistently high speed tires listeners and leaves no time for the message to sink in. I'll agree with those who recommend speaking slowly, but only when nervousness or trying to cover too much information has rushed the pace.

Speed Up

The problem with telling speakers to slow down is that it suggests that speaking slowly is the goal. It isn't. Using speed well is the goal. Adjusting the pace of your words to fit your message is an important part of performing a talk. Let's revisit the story from step 10: Gestures:

> *Our cats only go outside when we go outside. They behave like dogs, staying in the yard and coming in when called. One evening as we came in from eating on the patio, we called the cats, and they came bounding in. We didn't notice until she was inside that Cleo had a live mouse in her mouth. In hindsight, yelling, "Cleo, drop it!" was probably a bad idea, because now we had a mouse running around the dining room. For some reason, my wife got a broom and a dustpan; I got a small bucket.*

Madness ensued: The cats were skittering around the dining room batting at the mouse, my wife was poking at it with the broom and waving the dustpan around, and I was trying to drop the bucket on it every time it ran by me. After a few minutes, we cornered the mouse. Both cats were staring at it, Anne was holding the broom in the ready position, and I was sneaking up to it. I moved very slowly until the bucket was right over the mouse. Then, bam! I slammed down the bucket. Mouse captured.

This time, let's look at this story and focus on the speed of spoken words. By adjusting your pace as you tell the story it will be much more interesting.

I'd suggest reading these sentences in a slow, easy manner:

Our cats only go outside when we go outside. They behave like dogs, staying in the yard and coming in when called. One evening as we came in from eating on the patio, we called the cats, and they came bounding in. We didn't notice until she was inside that Cleo had a live mouse in her mouth.

Say these sentences at breakneck speed:

Madness ensued: The cats were skittering around the dining room batting at the mouse, my wife was poking at it with the broom and waving the dustpan around, and I was trying to drop the bucket on it every time it ran by me.

Speeding up helps listeners visualize the craziness. Changing the pace improves the telling of that story. However, varying speeds is important every time you speak, not just when you're telling stories. Even informational talks improve with variety. Some information is more important than other information, so slow down to emphasize it. Some information can be skimmed over, so you don't need to take as much time going through it. No matter the topic, a slow, steady pace can diminish audience interest just as much as having a monotonous voice. Change speeds to break the monotony and improve the listen-ability of all talks.

STOP

Many people are uncomfortable with silence. If a conversation pauses for a second or two, they get edgy and quickly try to restart it. I don't know where this aversion to silence comes from, but don't be afraid of it as a speaker. Pauses are powerful. They create anticipation, allowing listeners' imaginations to become active.

In hindsight, yelling, "Cleo, drop it!" was probably a bad idea, [Pause]

In that little space, the audience instantly starts thinking about all the different ways a mouse could cause problems if it had free rein in a house.

Pauses also make major points stand out:

The technology we are using will be totally outdated within five years. [Pause] Five years. [Pause] That's why we need to continue to innovate.

They also allow time for an emotional impact:

When the vet said that we had to put the dog down, we were devastated. Our cherished pet of 14 years would not be coming home with us. Devastated. [Pause]

It takes guts to pause and let silence rule. But silence does rule. Look at the faces of listeners when a speaker stops talking. All eyes are focused on that individual. No one looks away. Even people who weren't paying attention will zero in. Count in your head: Five years. [one one thousand, two one thousand, three one thousand] That's why. . . . At first, it will seem like the longest three seconds of your life. When you discover how much those three seconds will positively affect your message, you will be glad you invested the time.

◇◇

Key Points

- Don't race. Speaking at a sustained, high rate of speed tires listeners and diminishes your message.

- Don't speak slowly. Slow and steady lulls listeners to sleep.
- Change the pace. Speed up and slow down as you talk. Adjust pace to add excitement and emphasize key points.
- Pause. A complete stop will grab listeners and focus attention on the idea just presented.

Part 2 Postscript

As You Speak

If you compare the number of words in this book devoted to *creating a talk* with the number devoted to *performing a talk,* creating seems to have received more attention. Don't be fooled. While it is easier to describe the characteristics of performing, it's much more difficult to master performing them. You've likely developed habits in the way you present information, and breaking them will be difficult. You can rebuild PowerPoint slides overnight. Changing the way you present material will take continued commitment and practice.

Be assured that speaking skills can be learned and refined. You may think, "Some people are natural-born speakers, but not me." Nonsense. The way you speak is not determined at birth. While verbal communication may be easier for some, it doesn't mean you can't improve. Work on one element at a time. What would you most like to improve right now? What is the one piece that you think is holding you back? That is where you should start. Expect incremental progress—there is no, "Aha! Today is the day I got it!"—and try to improve every time you speak. At the next training session, add more life than you had the last time. At the next staff meeting, make it a goal to improve your eye contact. Take it one step at a time.

For some, performing will be a stretch. In her book *Quiet: The Power of Introverts in a World That Can't Stop Talking,* Susan Cain suggests that a third to half of us are introverts. She is in that group. You may be in that group. She brilliantly describes the characteristics of introverts and the pressures society places on them to become outgoing, hard-charging leaders. I passed the book's introvert test with flying colors, so as an introvert myself, I am not going to tell you that introversion is not OK or that you should become someone you aren't. However, I will point out that Cain is now on the lecture circuit, and I make my living as a speaker and consultant. How is that possible? Because *not being inclined* to do something is not the same as *not being able* to do something. You may find that performing a talk is a challenge, but one that is worth pursuing. You speak at your job. If you've ever had laryngitis, you know how important speech can be. I'd bet there are times you wish you were a little more outspoken. You don't have to become a new person. Just practice the skills you learn in this book.

For others, performing has always been part of their lives. They love being front and center. But your love of performing does not mean that everyone loves seeing you perform. You can continue refining your skills, too, so that you can be impressive while you are front and center.

Many years ago I introduced poise, voice, life, eye contact, gestures, and speed to an audience by writing those words on the chalkboard in the room. (Chalkboard? Yes, I told you it was many years ago.) One person called out from the back of the room, "P V Legs." Another acronym was born. I'm still surprised by the number of people who tell me they think about PVLEGS as they practice talking. If you think PVLEGS is a useful mnemonic device, please use it. If you are acronym-ed out, just remember the six steps.

Recall that the introduction to part 2 mentioned that how well you perform talks is more important than how well you create them. So many great messages are undercut or even lost because of poor delivery. If you focus on the six steps (PVLEGS), your performance skills will improve, and your listeners will be impressed.

Use this checklist to evaluate performance skills—your own and others.

Poise

- ☐ I appear calm and confident.
- ☐ There are no distracting behaviors.
- ☐ I recorded myself and watched for fidgeting, shuffling, and odd tics.

Voice

- ☐ My voice is just right for the space—not too loud or too soft.
- ☐ Every word can be heard.
- ☐ I don't mumble or blur words together.

Life

- ☐ I have feeling, emotion, and passion in my voice during the entire talk.
- ☐ Listeners can hear that I care about my topic.
- ☐ I have appropriate life in my voice. (Enthusiasm for things I am excited about; sadness for sad topics; anger for things I'm mad about.)

Eye Contact

- ☐ I look at every listener at some point during my talk.
- ☐ My eye contact is natural and fluid.
- ☐ If I use notes, I use them well. I only take quick glances to remind myself of key words.
- ☐ I talk to my audience, rather than read at them.

Gestures

- ☐ My hand gestures add to my words.
- ☐ Emphatic hand gestures make key points stand out.
- ☐ Descriptive hand gestures make it easy to visualize my talk.
- ☐ My face is full of expression. Facial gestures add to my words.
- ☐ Body gestures are effective. I lean in, shrug, and use other body motions to engage the audience.

Speed

☐ I use speed well. I speed up, slow down, and pause where appropriate to add to my message.

☐ I change pace for effect.

Part 3

Creating and Performing in Action

Simple. Practical. Understandable. These 11 steps will help you become an impressive speaker. If you create a talk using the five preparation steps and perform the talk using the six performance steps, you will be effective in all speaking situations. In part 3, you will find out how to apply these steps in digital presentations, the workplace, and social situations.

Remember, this is not a book about training, managing, selling, interviewing, podcasting, or becoming a professional speaker. There are many excellent books specifically devoted to each of those topics, as well as organizations that offer informative resources for those who want to continue developing their skills. This book is about speaking in general. Reading the workplace training section will not solve all your training problems, but it *will* help you become a more impressive speaker as you train. It will also help you assess your situation and needs so that you can evaluate materials for trainers differently and better. For example, "Ah, this is a book about visual aids. Our training materials really need improvement in that area." Or, "Here is a book with energizers and ways to open and close training sessions. We need to add this to our content." Or, "This book about presentations doesn't have anything about life. That's the thing we still need to work on, so let's look for another resource." Or, "Our training sessions are increasingly dominated by Millennials. How can we reach this audience? We need to find a book with specific ideas for reaching them."

Similarly, reading the managing section will not make you a great manager, but it will make you a better communicator as you manage. Remember, competently communicating bad strategies doesn't make them good strategies. You *will* be able to think differently about the management materials in the marketplace. For example, a book about measuring employee engagement is about audience. Your target market in this instance is your employees. Are you reaching them and engaging them? How can you understand more about them to be more effective? A program about building relationships is about audience and content. Who is on your team? What are their characteristics? What can you add to your communications to better connect with them?

On the personal level, as you develop your performance skills you will also be able to evaluate yourself better. You may discover that your biggest weakness is achieving poise. Look for resources that share strategies that help you relax and feel more confident. If you continue to struggle to add life to your talks, find resources that zoom in on that. My goal is to point you in the right direction, so you know exactly what to look for should you desire more in-depth work on one of the 11 steps.

All speaking situations are opportunities to use the framework introduced in parts 1 and 2. You create the message and you deliver the message every time you speak. Asking for a raise? Eleven steps to success. Making an instructional video? Eleven steps to success. Speaking at a graduation? Eleven steps to success. Giving the "State of the Union"? Eleven steps to success. That said, in some cases one or two steps may be especially important. For this reason, the following sections only address the steps that are particularly important for success in that area. For example, you may think "audience, content, organization, visual aids, and looks" as you read the section for managers, but I only discuss audience, content, visual aids, and life. That doesn't mean the others are not important for managers. I simply chose to highlight steps that require special consideration. For trainers, visual aids are critical, but I don't give them extra attention in the social talk discussion. All steps apply to all speaking situations, but some steps need to be highlighted in some situations. This book shares general tips, and you can also visit www.ownanyoccasion.com for examples and more ideas.

11-Step Speaking in the Digital World

It wasn't long ago that I used transparencies and an overhead projector when I presented. I used an easel with chart paper and a chalkboard as well. Times have changed quite a bit. Indeed, the world is changing so fast that it is dangerous to talk about digital tools in a print book. By the time the book goes to press, a website mentioned in the book may no longer exist. Some tools that were cutting edge may be yesterday's news. That's OK. I am more concerned with concepts—how to use the sites and the tools—than I am about any one website or device. If a website mentioned here disappears, a quick Internet search will help you find six other sites that serve the same purpose; if smartphones are replaced by geniusphones, you will be able to adapt the ideas I share for use with the new tools. If you are constantly striving to better your speaking skills and methods, you'll be fine.

Practicing Speaking

Before I show you how to use the 11 steps to produce better digital talks and presentations, I want to mention the websites and devices you can use to help you develop as a speaker. Remember being told to practice your school speeches in front of a mirror? It was a good way to practice and to see how you look to your audience. Fortunately, there are many ways now to practice your skills, gauge how you look, and receive feedback on your talks.

Some of you may remember camcorders: the large, heavy cameras we used to record video of the kids' soccer games and school plays. It's hard to believe that such unwieldy devices existed, right? Every device is a video recorder now. Apple computers have Photo Booth in the dock. A couple of clicks and you can use the built-in mic and camera to record video. Every PC has a built-in camera and mic, too. Tablets can record video, and so can smartphones. I can't count the number of times someone has held up an iPad, pointed it at me, and recorded me during workshops. Use your device's recording feature and point it at yourself as you rehearse. Watch the video and then rate yourself using the checklists at the end of part 1 and part 2. What are you doing well? What one area should you work on? Don't try to improve everything at once. Just focus on the most important change you need to make right now. Re-record. Did you improve?

There is a trick to self-evaluation. While some people are too generous with themselves and fail to notice their flaws, most of us are hyper-critical: "Is that what I sound like? Ugh!" "I look terrible." There is a reason that prominent actors and actresses are paid well: They look and sound terrific on screen. Most of us don't. Don't panic, you aren't competing with Hollywood's top stars. You are competing with yourself. Can you make your talk look and sound better than it did last time? But why stop at self-evaluation? Every recording can easily be shared with others, so enlist trusted friends and mentors to view your video and offer feedback.

If you are in the workplace, record yourself in action. You can hook up an inexpensive video camera to your laptop. Set one on a little tripod and point it at yourself as you lead the meeting or training session. How well did you create your talk? How well did you perform it? Brave presenters also point a camera at the audience occasionally. Was everyone engaged? Did you miss some audience reaction because you were busy presenting? Remember, all talks are designed for the audience. You may think you did well, but the faces in the audience may reveal otherwise, and their opinion is more important than yours.

While social speaking is usually a one-and-done event, you can still learn from recording yourself. Recording your talk at your son's bar mitzvah may not help you with the next bar mitzvah (unless you've got a second son). Still, you can review the recording to not only remember it, but also evaluate your speaking ability. Then you can apply what you've learned the next time you have the chance to speak socially.

Creating Digital Presentations

In workplace situations, many people are being asked to create virtual instruction for webinars, instructional videos, webcam chats, and video conferences. I'm sure you have witnessed some dreadful examples of digital presentations. At the end of part 1, I suggested creating your talk while thinking about audience, content, organization, looks, and visual aids. You can use the VOCAL steps to avoid adding to the dreadful example file. However, the tips in this section can be used beyond the workplace. I was at a wake for a good friend a short time ago, for example, where someone who could not attend in person submitted a video tribute. You, too, can speak at events virtually. The ideas in this section will help you create impressive videos.

I bet you can think of many different digital tools that can be used to broadcast or record and share verbal communication. Your company probably uses a large variety of tools internally, and you may use several options at home to talk to others (Skype and FaceTime, for example). No matter what tool you use, you must use it well. It doesn't matter which screen-casting software you use, which type of slides you create, or which movie-making software you have. If you don't pay attention to the five steps of creating, you may not succeed.

Audience

Who is the audience for your digital presentation? For in-person talks, the audience is limited and easy to identify. You know your staff, you know who has signed up for the training session, and you know who was invited to the wedding. Digital tools expand that audience. Think of a training video about email etiquette. Who will see it? Most instructional videos are generic and designed for no particular audience. They are so bland that they engage no viewers. You want to design your video in a way that engages all possible viewers. I'll discuss how to fix that in the content section, but you won't know what content to add if you don't know your entire audience.

Be conversational, because digital audiences tend to be casual. If they are sitting at home in their PJs drinking coffee while watching the final video to reach Gold Point Status on the company leaderboard, formal language will be off-putting. Listeners quickly leave unfriendly sounding places. Record yourself reading your material and then listen to the recording. Is it too formal? Will listeners be put off?

Content

How much time do you have? Much less than you think. You have heard that people, especially young people, spend massive amounts of time looking at their screens. However, they don't spend very much time looking at one thing on the screen. Digital viewers only "spend, on average, between 19 and 27 seconds looking at a page before moving on to the next one" (Carr 2011). There are just too many options to choose from. Devices are engaging, but it's challenging to make a podcast or video engaging.

Think of your own behavior. Have you ever attended a webinar? How long did it take before your mind wandered or you got up to get a snack and play with the dog? Have you ever sat down to watch a nine-minute video? After a minute and 57 seconds, you probably already thought that it was the longest video ever, right? Even highly entertaining music videos and cat-antic compilations are not watched to the end. If you think folks will spend a solid 45 minutes watching your online conflict-management training session or your family history video, you are mistaken. Put your content into very short chunks.

It is easy to connect with a person right in front of you. Proximity alone creates a relationship. Online, however, all personal connection is lost because the human element is gone. Good digital presentations need to be full of connectors, which are direct, obvious statements that connect your topic to your listeners' lives and connect you to your listeners. Let's look at a couple of examples.

Think about an online training session about email etiquette. The odds are excellent that the examples will include generic and boring email addresses like john.doe@anywhereUSA and jane.doe@anywhereUSA. Instead, create a connection by using actual email addresses from your company.

> *Anna in the San Antonio Lennox office had a question about how to look up parts and contacted the Orlando office. Let's use her email, a.wisneski@lennox.com, as the sample address.*

If you can't personalize within the video because it is from a third-party developer, personalize with an added video you create. Perhaps someone from your company can introduce the training video and include something specific about how it applies to your company.

Sending a video for a social situation? Use your audience analysis to connect with those attending. "I know you are there, Jana, so you can back me up on this. Remember when. . . . " This turns a "talking at the wedding couple" video into "talking to the couple and guests" video.

Organization

Before I entered the site at Climax Molybdenum Mine that I talked about in step 4, I had to watch a video about mine safety. The video probably cost a lot of money to make, and I'm sure that well-meaning professionals put it together. Watching it, though, I was struck by its lack of organization. The video had no structure and randomly jumped from rules about driving around the site to weather issues in the mountains to how to clean up a spill to health problems caused by high altitude to warning horns heard before blasting to required PPE (personal protective equipment) to how to report an accident. It was 20 minutes of various bits of information. The lack of organization made it difficult to remember anything, and

I bet that if I had been given a quiz about the 11 topics covered, I wouldn't have passed.

In this case, it would have been helpful to chunk the content to avoid losing the audience's attention. Chunking content also serves as a memory aid because you can put similar items together and then use signposts:

> *This part of the video is about the personal matters of PPE and high-altitude health. Next we'll move on to concerns when you are outside the offices, including driving around the site, avoiding dangerous weather, and knowing about blasting. Finally, we'll look at accident procedures for dealing with spills and reporting injuries.*

I wouldn't have had to remember 11 different items, but rather three different chunks. Then, if I had been given a quiz about the three parts and the content in each one, I bet I would have passed. Chunking information and being explicit about the organization helps all presentations. It is especially crucial in screening situations, where minds are more prone to wandering.

Some companies have a bigger organization problem: How should all the digital information be organized? There may be information in the corporate learning management system (LMS), in the content management system (CMS), on third-party sites, on knowledge management systems (KMS), in SharePoint, and in other places. Your company may have massive amounts of helpful information for newly onboarded employees, for example, but can they find it? Conversations you want to avoid:

> *I spent all afternoon looking online to figure out how to clean the fan filter.*
>
> *You did? We already have that information.*
>
> *Where?*

The beauty of the Internet is that in a couple of clicks, we can find what we need. Algorithms have made it possible to categorize and organize enormous amounts of information. Google will not sell you the algorithms they use, so you must create your own system to index information.

As you create digital content, create a system for intelligently storing and accessing it.

Looks

Before I speak, I choose an outfit that fits the occasion and makes me look good. Of course, appearance involves more than how I look. The audience will also notice the things around me. What does the venue look like? I have given talks in some strange places and on some strange stages. I can't control that.

When you point a camera at yourself, the audience will also see more than your personal appearance. What surrounds you? In this case, you *can* control that. Take some tips from Hollywood. Before the camera starts rolling, a set designer has very carefully made sure everything in the frame is perfect. How does your set look? If you do a webcast from your office, will viewers see piles of papers on your desk? Does the camera show old, stained ceiling tiles? Will viewers know that you had a sub and chips for lunch?

In Hollywood, there are experts who set up lights in a special way—no face is dimly lit or hard to see, and nothing in the background is lit in a way that takes attention off the actors. Pay attention to the type of light. I move lamps around before I do webinars because the lamp I like for deskwork makes me look pale and sickly.

Hollywood also has makeup artists and stylists who make the actors look better. You probably won't take things that far, but you might. When I was asked to make an instructional video for ASCD, a global leader in developing and delivering materials for educators, I expected someone with a camera to follow me around as I worked. I did not expect to have a makeup artist. At first I was worried about the "lipstick on a pig" cliché, but when I saw the final product I could see how the makeup counteracted the effect of bright lights. My point? Do extra things to make yourself look good on a close-up camera.

Take a screen shot before you hit record. Study that shot, and make changes to ensure that the camera captures the best possible picture.

Visual Aids

How important are first impressions? Very. In just a few seconds, we form opinions about the people we meet, and those opinions are long lasting. First impressions apply in the digital world, too. Within a few seconds of clicking on your digital creation, viewers will judge it. How can you ensure that those judgments are positive? Apply the concepts that we discussed in step 5.

Give special consideration to accessibility. How will viewers see your video, webinar, or webcast? If it is projected onto a large screen in the training room or at the reception hall, then your standard presentation will work. But what about when your product is seen on the screen of a computer, laptop, tablet, or smartphone? Will it work then? You need to adapt your images and text for a small screen. Don't assume that a slide that works well on a six-foot screen will work on a six-inch screen. A graph will work much better when projected onto a large screen in the lecture hall than it will on a smartphone, small laptop, or tablet. Think of how your visuals will look on the small screen and make adjustments. Maybe one slide with four images should be broken into four slides; maybe the labels on the pie chart should be enhanced. For many, size-eight fonts are unreadable, especially on a six-inch tablet. Viewers shouldn't struggle trying to read microscopic text. You should also think about simplicity. A complex diagram is indecipherable on a four-inch screen, and people won't notice the details in an image. View anything you create on the device that your audience will use. Do all the visuals work?

In the digital world, the term *visual aids* is anachronistic. Your web-based productions will probably have audio aids as well. I'll point out that the same concerns exist with audio as with visual aids. How will listeners hear you? On large speakers broadcast throughout the conference room or on a device's tiny speakers? Remember that sound may not be as clear on the smaller speakers.

A bigger issue is poorly chosen sound. For example, podcast creation software makes it easy to add a looping soundtrack. You can select a clip of various lengths (10 seconds, 20 seconds, and so on) and have the clip repeat automatically for the duration of your video. Do some math. If you use a 10-second clip in a four-minute video, listeners will hear that music sample 24 times! They will grow tired of it no matter how fun you thought it was when you selected it. Random looping soundtracks also become annoying—you don't need nonstop music. Remember how powerful a pause is when you speak? A break from music is a good idea, too. If you want to include music, choose something that adds to the mood you are trying to create with your words. A cute jingle does not enhance serious words.

Performing for Digital Presentations

Poise, voice, life, eye contact, gestures, and speed are the six steps to performing successful talks. Digitally shared talks are no exception. Poise, voice, and speed don't require much new thinking, but it is good to remember a few specifics. Cameras can reveal odd tics, so make sure you're poised before you hit the record button. Making every word heard can be a problem, especially if small speakers are the main way your learners hear you, so make sure your recording volume levels are appropriate. Small speakers also require you to think about speed differently—when you record, speak a bit slower than you might in person. If you speed up to create excitement, make sure your words are still distinct.

Life, eye contact, and gestures deserve a bit more discussion.

Life

Recall that adding life is the number one way to engage listeners, yet it is also the number one weakness of most speakers. Unfortunately, recordings demand even more life than live presentations. I once had a chance to audition for commercials for a local business. The director did not look at me standing on the spot with bright lights in my face. Instead, he sat in the dark at the back of the room and watched my image on the small screen. He used headphones to hear how I would sound through the microphone. Why? Because there is a huge difference between how people look and sound in-person and how they look and sound in media. Media deadens us. To seem excited on TV about the big sale required much more life than I ever imagined.

In step 8, I suggested using a 1 to 10 scale. But with recordings, your score will be lowered by three points, so you need to factor that in. If you are at level 6 when you record, you will sound like level 3 during playback. If you are at level 5 as you do your conference call, listeners will hear level 2 and will be unimpressed. Actors get paid well because they can bump it up a notch—or three. You must do the same to be effective with digital tools. In the old days, people worried about wasting film. That isn't the case now. You can record and re-record and re-record, making sure that every recording has more life than the last. Someone listening in-person as you record might think you sound over-the-top. Good! That will play back nicely.

Eye Contact

Most computers put the lens for their built-in cameras at the top-center of the screen. That's why you notice foreheads when you use tools such as Skype. Because we stare at ourselves onscreen, the camera angle makes it seem like we are looking slightly down. Hence, our foreheads are on display.

Make sure you know where the camera lens is and look directly at it. Think "camera contact," not eye contact. You "look at" your audience by looking at the lens. If you are recording a message, never take your eyes off the lens. You don't need to worry about how you look. Just know that watching yourself onscreen as you record will make you look worse. If you are in a videoconference or similar, look at the screen to watch others as they speak, but then look at the camera when it is your turn. Making this small adjustment will make you seem much more engaging and impressive than everyone else online.

Gestures

What does the camera see? What gestures will be in the frame? Don't stop using your hands, but be aware of whether people will see them. In a training room or onstage, I'll sometimes point at part of the screen to call out something I don't want the audience to miss. In the digital world, you may need to use a digital gesture—an onscreen pointer, perhaps—to serve that function.

While it isn't required to have the camera close to you, that seems to be the most common setup for screencasts and the like. For close-camera video recording, the most important gestures will be your facial gestures. Try watching a movie without sound and studying the faces of the actors. Notice how many subtle and not-so-subtle facial movements they make. They are able to express every little emotion—some tiny, short-lived squint reveals "I doubt it." A small side glance suggests "I don't trust you." People notice little gestures and they have an impact. At a minimum, make sure your face reveals that you are passionate about what you are saying. Work on using your face as actors do to communicate even without words.

Putting It All Together

It's all common sense, right? I don't think I have recommended anything that is particularly trendy, avant-garde, or out of the ordinary. But as you know, common sense is not always very common. Look at every webinar, video, podcast, and videoconference you watch with new eyes. Critique what you see using the 11-step framework. How well was the product created? Thinking about audience, content, organization, visual and other aids, and looks will help you analyze mistakes that are frequently made and avoid them.

How well did the speakers perform? Awareness of poise, voice, life, camera contact, gestures, and speed will make you more impressive than many speakers you will see on YouTube. In a world where vocal communication is on display in so many ways, it surprises me that so many people have neglected to develop their core speaking skills.

Don't hit record until you have created a message worth recording and worked on a performance worth watching. Don't enter into virtual conversations until you have put yourself in a position to succeed onscreen with strong verbal skills to showcase. Simple steps that others have ignored will make your digital presence powerful and will make you successful.

13

11-Step Speaking in Training

If you're a trainer, use the 11-step framework to evaluate training sessions differently. If they haven't been going as well as you'd like, ask if the problem is in how the materials were created or how the materials were delivered. Was the training session perfectly designed for the audience, with appropriate, important, and engaging content? Was it well organized? Did the visual aids impress? Yes? Then the trainers must have fallen down on some element of performing. Can you think of a trainer or training session that stands out? Did the training session get results because of how it was put together? If so, create other training sessions that way. Is it because the trainer excelled at delivering the course? If so, teach other trainers how to perform that well.

One of the strangest compliments I ever received was from an attendee at a training session I once did in Michigan. After I was finished, he came up and said, "I couldn't get anything done during your talk. I just had to pay attention!" I was flattered by the remark, but I quickly realized the dark side of his comment. His expectation was that he would be able to check email, do some paperwork, and probably play Angry Birds during the session.

Years of experience had taught him that most talks, training sessions, or workshops have small moments of value followed by lots of "I don't need to pay attention to this." That's a pretty low expectation. How can that be changed?

One company that is ahead of the curve is Freeport-McMoRan (FMI). It recognized this problem and hired me to develop a speaking course for training the trainers. As with many companies, FMI promotes excellent employees into training roles. Most of those employees didn't initially know much about educational methods or instructional design, but FMI had courses to help them learn about these topics. FMI realized, though, that those courses were not enough—the trainers would be more effective if they were better communicators.

You may not have the luxury of taking a company-provided course. However, being well spoken and improving your communication skills will make you a more effective trainer. As you read this section, you may realize that you want to learn more about some areas. Don't worry, there are many training resources out there. For example, there are books about reaching the Millennial audience, adding interaction to your content, or designing slides for visual aids. Use the 11-step framework to assess your needs and point yourself in the right direction.

Creating a Training Session

What must be done before your training session? VOCAL preparation! Focusing on just one piece—content—is all too common. You have your topic—information protection, conflict management, proper food storage, credit union regulations, designing virtual training, diversity training, HIPAA rules—and all you have to do is give the required content to the attendees, right? Not exactly.

Audience

The content is the content, and you have to cover it no matter who is attending. Sadly, too many trainers have that attitude. Let's assume here that your goal is to do more than simply cover the content, however. You want to see results. The problem is that what works for some people does not work for others. Find out what makes your trainees tick and adjust your session to their needs.

Unfortunately, you may be starting in a hole because training often has a bad reputation. What do employees think when they hear, "Block out next Tuesday for training?" Without even knowing the topic, their first reaction is "Ugh." They'll probably assume it's going to be an unproductive experience, time they would rather have to address the work piling up while they are in the training session. Is the training session compulsory or voluntary? If compulsory, the hole may be even deeper. "We have to be here" is much worse than "We want to be here."

Adding to this is a level of suspicion: "Are you someone who knows my business?" "Do you have tips for my life?" Barb Rarden, a consultant with Teradata, puts it this way: "Trainers of adults can never presume they are teaching blank slates. They must learn to overcome cynicism and engineer trust in the room before taking a first step into transferring knowledge. Adults come into training with much baggage about learning environments and a space must be carved through all that in order to create a willingness to learn."

Know that you will need to add content to address cynicism before you even get to your topic. Add content to sell yourself, explaining your expertise and your connection to their situation. Then, add content to sell the training session, explaining how it will improve their performance and workplace.

Margaret McGuckin works with companies struggling with growth and implementation problems. As chief operating officer, she helped Clear-Choice Dental Implant grow from a $1 million company to a $135 million company in four years, doing a lot of training along the way. She refers to some training sessions as "Mug of the Month" sessions. These are the ones that employees recognize as failing to address bigger issues and, frankly, as gimmicky. They don't trust that what you are presenting is worthwhile. I like to sneak a peek through the "Employees Only" door to look in the back rooms of stores where I shop. I always see signs posted from the latest inspirational or motivational program presented and a clever acronym or slogan pinned to the corkboard. Check for similar evidence wherever you train. It may help you find out whether your audience has a "And now what?" or "You again?" attitude.

When Dan trains the electricians at his company, he sometimes has classes with a mix of first-year apprentices, journeymen, and master electricians with 16 years of experience. To make the training program as effective as possible, he needs to be aware of different levels of knowledge in the room. You may be in a similar position at your company. So what do you do?

The first step is to use the experience information you gained when you analyzed your audience to adjust the content as needed. For example, Dan had to add some explanations that wouldn't have been necessary if all trainees were journeymen or master electricians. Next, adjust your schedule. Dan gave the experienced electricians an extra break while he explained the terms to the apprentices. Finally, be willing to give up some control and use any in-class experts. Dan lets the master electricians teach, following Barlo's suggestion that "trainers need to discover the wisdom and expertise in the audience and pull it out." If you know there are experts in your class, adjust your content again. You don't need to present all the information. The experts in the room from the client's organization would probably love to share, and their co-workers will give one of their own immediate credibility. Opportunities of this type improve the organization, too: "Employees at high performance organizations are four times more likely to share knowledge with their colleagues as workers at low-performance companies" (Cole 2016). Find out who is in the room so you can facilitate that sharing.

Do your trainees like classrooms? I ask this because I know many people like Dave, who hated high school. The minute he got his diploma, he was done with schooling. He loved working with his hands and became an extremely successful drywaller. People loved his work, he was in high demand, and he started hiring others. Before long, he oversaw a large business and had new employees to train. Dave guessed that they probably liked traditional classroom environments as much as he did. When he hired someone to come in and discuss safety concerns, Dave requested changes to the presentation: less reading onscreen text, not as much lecture time, more images from work sites, and less seat time. And the large binder for each trainee? The thing that no one will ever open once the training is done? Don't bother. The information is on-site and supervisors are aware of the issues, so let's not waste money on 25 binders. Dave wanted experiential learning, not classroom learning, for his audience.

Dave and his employees are not alone. Other groups—Millennials, for instance—dislike classrooms as well. Generalizations are dangerous, and to say all Millennials dislike classrooms is apt to be met with examples of Millennials who love classes, but growing up in the digital age has certainly influenced the group that now makes up 35 percent of the workforce (Fry 2015). For one, they are used to accessing any information they want anytime they want. They believe that they don't need a class; they just need the Internet to find an instructional YouTube video. Young people may be thinking, "Why do I need you?" Answer that question. Break through the initial cynicism by adding your real-life experience. Explain to Millennials that everything cannot be found online. Explain the expertise you have that they can't get on YouTube. Show them that there is power in learning from you, the trainer. Sell yourself to them.

Barb, Margaret, Dan, and Dave know that successful training starts with understanding those who are being trained. You should follow their examples.

Content

Bob Pike runs a company that has been training trainers for decades. He asks an interesting question: Do you have the right content to accomplish your goal? He tells a story about a trainer who comes in to teach about stress management and offer tips about how to reduce stress in your life.

Noble goals to be sure, but that training session failed to explore *why* people were stressed. What if the stress is caused by too many impossible-to-meet deadlines? After the trainer's session, Pike figures that employees still won't be able to meet deadlines, but now they simply won't care. Is that the goal?

Or, consider a training session for call center workers. These usually involve handing out a script with conversational branches that share what to say when certain types of customers are on the phone. But what if the workers are ineffective not because they don't have the right material but because they are boring? What if they don't need new scripts but rather lessons about learning proper speaking skills, specifically voice and life? Make sure the content presented gets to the root of the problem.

Assuming you have the right content, take some time to answer these questions:

- Will this help me on the job?
- How will this affect the results I need to get?
- What does this offer that I can't get from on-the-job training?
- Why do I need you to train me?

Finally, think about the type of content to add. Good training sessions include variety. Don't be fooled into believing that there is only one type of acceptable content. Lecture has a bad connotation, yet TED Talks are enormously popular. Why? Because good lecturers impart valuable information quickly. Don't rule out traditional presentation methods. Training in the actual workplace environment is great, but if that isn't possible, simulations can give the feel of real-life experiences. Build interactive activities into your content, allowing trainees to engage with the learning and with one another. After presenting a small chunk of content, give the audience a chance to do something with that information.

TMI

TMI means "too much information." I know that you have too much information in your training. It's a bold statement, but I am confident making it because I have years of experience and have watched hundreds of training sessions. Remember the man in Oakland who said he would speak as fast as possible to cover everything? He has too much information for the time provided, but believes that it's all worthwhile. It doesn't matter; something must go.

When I was in education, the Smarter Balanced Assessment Consortium (SBAC) was developing year-end tests that were aligned with the Common Core State Standards many states had adopted. The thinking was that all schools should use the same test to accurately compare students across the country. Educators wanted to know if there were multiple-choice questions, short answer questions, constructed response questions, and so on. So, someone from SBAC made a presentation to show us what the test would look like. During the presentation, we were told that the test was created by work groups consisting of "six or more members from advisory or governing states, one liaison from the executive committee, and one WestEd partner." No one cared, no one knew what that meant, and no one remembered that information seconds after the slide was gone. Worse, no one believed that information would contribute to preparing students for the test.

Your trainees don't need all the information in your training session either. Do a web search of the forgetting curve. You'll find many studies that attempt to discover how much people remember after instruction. One study shows that within one hour, people will have forgotten an average of 50 percent of the information you presented. Within 24 hours, they have forgotten an average of 70 percent of new information, and within a week, forgetting claims an average of 90 percent of it (Kohn 2014).

People do not typically forget information they need, so there must be a lot of nonessential content in these training sessions. Be thorough when you review the material you plan to include. Do all attendees need all of it?

Investigate Microlearning

We think of training in large blocks: a 90-minute e-learning module, four hours with a trainer, or two days off-site. Microlearning, on the other hand, delivers training content in very small increments. Chunks of five or 10 minutes are easier to fit into busy schedules. Think of a training program based on this book. Yes, it could be presented in the four- or eight-hour training sessions I'm typically scheduled for, but it could also be broken into small pieces presented digitally. For example, the visual aid help in step 5 could be presented in five, 5-minute pieces: how to be on point, crucial, accessible, simple, and multimedia inclusive. Using speed well in step 11 could become three, 5-minute sections: slowing down, changing pace, and pausing.

Over time—at times convenient for the trainees—all the pieces needed to be an effective speaker would be presented. Will microlearning work for all content? No. But it might work for some audiences and some topics. Add it to your training arsenal.

Avoid Fads

Be careful about choosing trendy over effective. For instance, kids today love games, right? Based on that belief, if you turn your diversity training into a game it will be a big hit. Or will it? As I was writing this book, the augmented reality game Pokémon Go was released. Everywhere I went, I saw groups of 15- to 35-year-olds walking around outside with their faces glued to their smartphone screens. It wasn't the beautiful sunset that drew crowds to the pier in Victoria, British Columbia; it was Pokémon nearby that the game creators placed in the water. You know what else I saw around that time? Many articles for trainers and educators about how to use the Pokémon Go model to alter instruction. Two months after the game was released, however, articles were coming out about the large number of players leaving the game. A third of active users have already quit playing.

There is a cautionary tale here: Games come and go. Trying to invent a game that will last is a difficult task. Gamification is hot, but likely only for a limited time. Avoid jumping on training bandwagons.

Add Follow-Up Content

Training sessions are not an event; they are a journey. Think about the speaking-skills training that I offer, for example. In a four-hour training session, I can introduce the 11 steps and offer guided practice, but trainees won't master speaking in that time. So in addition, I provide digital tools for continuing the training asynchronously afterward. Explore and use different types of e-learning platforms to add post-training information and refreshers.

Visual Aids

Reread step 5. Trainers tend to be slide bound more than other speakers, so what was said there is more important to you than it might be to others. If you are creating materials for your training session, follow the ideas presented there.

Your training aids should be based on your answer to the question, "What will trainees have trouble with?" That is not the same as, "Is everything I am going to present on the slides?" Of course, if everything is on the slides, you can kill two birds with one stone: Create a presentation and the trainee notebook at the same time! Make your slides as dense as a textbook, turn them into a PDF file, punch three holes in each page, and call it a training binder, right? Efficient! And doubly wrong. Trainees do not want to see a textbook on screen. They do not want to read a notebook filled with pictures of 144 PowerPoint slides. But what if you print the slides with lines next to them for taking notes? Three birds with one stone! Creating pages of indecipherable pictures of densely packed slides made even smaller so you can accommodate some lines for notes that will never be taken is a bad idea. Make presentation materials that stand out and that address areas where trainees might have problems. Technical training sessions require more information than motivational training sessions, so yes, in those cases there will be more slides and information in the deck. In general, though, less is more.

Many trainers do not have the option to create their own materials because they're given an entire package to use for the session. For example, when Katie trained the nursing staff about pressure ulcer prevention, she was told to use the PowerPoint deck that previous trainers had used. She knew there were problems with the materials. Every slide had bullet points—even a slide with only one sentence on it. She took out the bullet points. Many slides had text and a small picture that was vital to understanding the content in the upper right-hand corner. She decided to take the text off the slide and make the image much larger. In design terminology, she made full-bleed images and then added a little text on top of the image. Katie also deleted any slides that had information trainees didn't need—slides with information they already knew and slides with information they didn't need to know. Her supervisor was impressed. Katie may have gone out on a limb changing the training session without permission, but her courage led to good results and good reviews from her boss.

Consider tweaking the material given to you. Removing text and replacing it with an image may not be allowed by your employer, but other adjustments might be possible. For example, take a dense slide and turn it into three slides that are easier to read. See Figure 13-1.

Figure 13-1. Overloaded and Balanced Training Slides

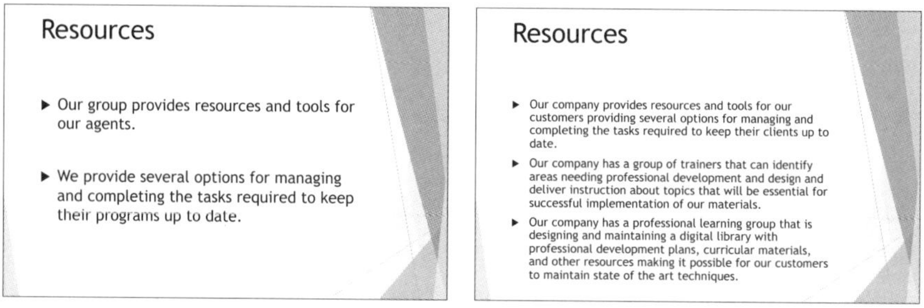

Resources

- Our group provides resources and tools for our agents.

- We provide several options for managing and completing the tasks required to keep their programs up to date.

Resources

- Our company provides resources and tools for our customers providing several options for managing and completing the tasks required to keep their clients up to date.

- Our company has a group of trainers that can identify areas needing professional development and design and deliver instruction about topics that will be essential for successful implementation of our materials.

- Our company has a professional learning group that is designing and maintaining a digital library with professional development plans, curricular materials, and other resources making it possible for our customers to maintain state of the art techniques.

Consider changing image size and placement. Put text on top of an image. Saying "look at the picture above and notice the difference" does not work as well as writing "this is the difference" right on the image. If allowed, replace some text with an image. (But be aware of copyright! Searching Google Image and pasting the first picture you find into your show may not be legal.) Be bold and make the changes your trainees will appreciate.

Performing When You Are Training

Everything discussed so far is about what you need to do before the training. Creating great training materials is essential, but it's not sufficient for success. You know that poorly delivered training sessions are a problem; that's where PVLEGS comes in. You must be poised, have a voice that's easily heard, look at each trainee equally, use gestures, and adjust your speed. This is true for all speakers. However, when training, one performance aspect deserves extra attention: Life.

Life

What if your audience is unenthused? They may not want to be there. If you are monotonous in your training delivery, you will amplify their desire to be someplace else. At a technical training session where trainees need to learn the information, poor performance may be tolerated because the trainees are motivated by the content. Trainers who add life to their talk will make the day more enjoyable, but trainees are willing to suffer through a presenter's monotony because they must master the content. They may think, "I have to learn how the new software works despite how bad you are." It's not desirable, but it's workable.

For the most part, though, education is about engagement. So how do you make a difficult topic such as compliance training engaging? One option is to use better aids and avoid bullet points. But the most effective way to engage your audience is by being more dynamic. Trainees may never be excited about a mandatory training session, but they should be excited about you.

Adding life means you must have variety (a range of feelings from seriousness to excitement), passion (evidence that what you're presenting matters), and warmth (feeling that trainees are valued). Trainees take their cue from you. If you sound excited, they will be excited. The excitement in your voice must be genuine and appropriate. And I'll repeat what I said earlier: Work on showing how passionate you are about the topic you're training people on. It is occasionally difficult for some speakers to maintain interest in their own talk. Think of a trainer who has presented the same topic a hundred times. They used to be passionate about the words and the topic, but not anymore. Your audience will always notice if you're simply going through the motions. If you train a lot, monitor yourself. If you find that your energy level is slipping, find ways to get back to the level of life you once had.

Finally, monitor your tone of voice. You can say, "You still don't get this?" in a way that conveys, "What are you, idiots? You still don't get this?" as well as in a way that says, "Hmm, you still don't get this? How can I help?" You can say, "This is the annual refresher on OSHA regulations" in a way that says, "I don't want to be here either," as well as in a way that says, "Let's do this!" Choose your tone of voice consciously. Be aware of what the life in your voice is doing to your words.

Digital Considerations

Look back at chapter 12's tips about giving digital presentations. The ideas there also apply to training environments (as well as the caution that websites come and go). However, some specific digital tools are also worth mentioning here.

Adding to In-Person Training

If there aren't many people in your training session, it's easy to personally interact with the trainees. For larger training sessions, however, you'll need to use digital tools to achieve interaction. You may already have tools to accomplish the purposes I describe, but there are also many free or inexpensive tools available. UMU is a site that allows you to poll the audience, check for understanding, and generate discussion by asking audience members to use their mobile devices to answer questions. TodaysMeet provides a back channel during your presentation where trainees can interact with one another in real time as you present to ask questions and share insights about the material presented. You can also check the back channel to see if there are any issues you need to address. However, keep in mind that participants may focus on the back channel rather than on you, so use this tool carefully.

Introduce and Follow Up on Your Training

One way to introduce your training session is with an online discussion board. I use VoiceThread before training sessions to get a sense of my audience and to start them thinking. I'll create a thread and record a video to start a discussion. Trainees can then watch my prompt and respond by typing, recording an audio or video response, or uploading some other material. All the responses will show up on the thread so you (and they) can interact with one another asynchronously. If you know how to use the tools in LinkedIn, you can create a discussion forum to accomplish the same purpose.

Don't forget to follow up on your training session. We know that once trainees leave the room, the information leaves their heads, so require post-training responses. Padlet is a site that lets you create an online bulletin board. You set a prompt, send out a link to the board, and have trainees post digital sticky notes to the board. Those notes could be audio responses, video responses, images, or uploaded tdocuments that include feedback about the training session, questions that come up after the session, or examples of how they've been using what they learned on the job. For instance, if I want to find out whether people are adding more life to their voices, I could put up a small phrase that calls for lots of life ("Don't let the dog eat that!") and require audio responses. As another example, a technical trainer may record a video of someone on the job, post the video, and ask trainees to evaluate the work done.

Improving Online Instruction

Do not assume that you can take the materials you use in the training room or conference center and simply put them into a digital platform. Many trainers believe that to flip instruction, all you need to do is use screen capture software (Camtasia, Adobe Captivate, Screencast-O-Matic) to record the same presentation done live. They forget that what works in person will not work as well in an e-learning or mobile learning situation.

Think for a minute about the millions of options available to someone online. Would you sit and watch pictures of computer screens, or would you choose amusing dog videos or sports highlights? You must design with devices in mind. Is the e-learning course you're designing for hospital employees about recognizing child abuse going to be taken at computer learning stations, or is it a mobile learning course that they can access from any device at any time? What works in a controlled environment on a large screen may not work when accessed on the light rail with a smartphone.

Add Social Media Platforms to Online Presentations

Create a discussion board online where listeners can react to the content and one another. Offer a hashtag on Twitter so learners can respond and interact with a larger audience (Readers of this book can use the Twitter account I created: @OwnAnyOccasion). Simulate a live presentation. Add a video of yourself to your e-learning class to make it seem as if it were in real time instead of static and prerecorded. Bring in entertaining elements—something fun about the company or the topic. Your training session may never compete with the entertaining choices and distractions on the web, but you can create digital instruction that is much better than what is typically seen.

11-Step Speaking for Managers

As I mentioned in the section for trainers, you can also use creating and performing as a context for understanding management. What are your needs? Are you competent creating your messages? Do you understand your audience (employees) and know how to engage and motivate them? Is your content full of good ideas that everyone agrees on? Are you well organized? If customers and employees look around the workplace, will it be visually appealing? Do you look sharp? Are you competent delivering your messages? Do your poise, voice, and life impress your co-workers? Are you comfortable looking people in the eye? Do you use gestures and speed well to enhance your words?

If so, you will be successful. Let's look at a few tips that will help you become even more successful.

Creating a Talk

Before you speak and as you speak: These are the two parts of all vocal communication. Managers often don't have a lot of time to prepare the talk. Much of what you do is on the fly, as you react and respond to customers and employees. Good managers anticipate situations and think about what they will say if certain events occur.

Audience

It is difficult to analyze an audience, even an audience of one. Case in point: Have you totally figured out your spouse, significant other, parent, or teenager? If the audience has more than one member, the analysis becomes even harder. Because our job as speakers is to reach every audience member, we have to make the effort.

But what if you have two audiences instead of one? Welcome to the world of most managers. One audience is the employees; the other, the superiors. The school principal must address the staff working for her while thinking about the superintendent and school board above her. The manager at Starbucks must be effective with the employees at his store, but also think about the district and regional managers. What if what the staff wants is at odds with the orders from above? Say that the district just purchased a new math program, but the teachers love the old one. Perhaps you remember when corporate Starbucks asked employees to talk with customers about race, but the baristas and the customers were extremely uncomfortable doing so (Mainwaring 2015).

How can you win with the audience you report to as well the audience that reports to you? Sometimes you can't. When that happens, be honest about it and move on. Sometimes you'll end up playing "Whose side are you on?" Successful managers need to lean toward the employees. Richard Branson once said, "Put your staff first, customers second, and shareholders third" (Raymundo 2014). Why? "If you look after your staff, they'll look after your customers. It's that simple" (Branson 2014). It is easier to defend yourself if your numbers are good, and your employees are the key to good numbers.

There is an inevitable us versus them attitude with employees. A manager who comes into the company from outside gets more of that attitude than someone who is promoted from within, but even then, it is amazing how fast you can go from "one of us" to "one of them." You'll make the problem worse if you distance yourself from them by putting up communication barriers. Mikael Cho (2016), for example, writes about the need to allow employees to be impolite. He argues that managers may make employees believe some comments are not allowed. "If one of my teammates feels it's easier to speak his or her mind with a friend than with me, we've failed," he says. Open communication is a great predictor of organizational success. Work to defeat the idea that "I can't tell her that because she is one of them." Build trust.

If you know your employees, you can capitalize on their strengths. Who can be given more freedom? Who has great ideas? It also gives you the ability to allow role shaping. For example, your employees' jobs may require writing specifications and interacting with clients, but one employee loves writing and another loves interacting. Let them adjust their responsibilities to match their talents and interests. If you know your employees, you can also support their needs. Do you have introverts working for you? Extroverts? Do they have problems working together? Offer training to help. If you know your employees, you will be able to mitigate their weaknesses. Who needs more encouragement? Who needs more individual attention? Respond to each employee differently depending on their needs. Know that there is a difference between treating everyone fairly and treating everyone equally.

Consider Brad. He has been the regional sales leader for Jos. A. Banks for three years in a row. When the store manager announces that someone from corporate is coming to train about a new sales program that should help employees increase their gross sales, he says that attendance is mandatory for everyone but Brad. This treatment may be unequal, but it's fair. Make sure you treat everyone in the top sales leaders category the same and everyone in the emerging sales leaders category the same way. Be fair with your employees.

Content

Think about how often you hear "Not another meeting!" from your employees. According to EventBoard's inaugural "Employee Happiness

Survey," nearly 60 percent of working professionals spend one to two hours a day in meetings; 75 percent of midmanagement employees and above spend three to four hours in meetings (Teem 2016). In other words, a large part of your content seems to be shared at meetings. But the same survey showed that 41 percent of workers miss meetings "somewhat often" due to other commitments, and 56 percent say meetings that run long are a source of workplace conflict. If workers can frequently miss meetings and still perform on the job, were the meetings critical? Were they even worthwhile?

Have you ever missed a two-hour meeting and had a co-worker fill you in about what you missed? How long did that take? Ten minutes? That meeting had a lot of fat, didn't it? Re-examine your meetings. Be ruthless in critiquing their content. Cut the fat. And if you want to eliminate workplace conflict, pick the low-hanging fruit: End meetings on time. End meetings early and create good will! The simplest content adjustment managers can make is to control meetings well.

Review all the comments you make in a day, verbally or in writing, and categorize them: giving orders, giving assistance, assigning tasks, explaining why we're doing this, explaining how to do this, setting expectations, fixing, praising, encouraging, reprimanding, or whatever other categories you think apply. What did you find? This gives you a picture of who you are as a manager. You are your content as far as your employees are concerned. There is no "I think I am a nice guy, but they don't get me" escape. If you don't like what you see, adjust your content.

You should also add content to meet the needs of your employees. You cannot expect them to succeed at tasks they are unprepared to do. For example, Margaret McGuckin believes that Millennials spend "so much time in front of screens that social skills are lacking." As a manager, you need to be a role model for social skills, but perhaps you also need to add "improved oral communication" to your expectations and provide help for your employees. And while we're on the subject of Millennials, know that they want regular, constant feedback and career advice. The annual or semiannual review model is outdated. If talent development is your goal, don't wait six months or a year to reveal a person's strengths and weaknesses. How about now?

If you are going through big changes, communicate every move to your employees. In a survey by Robert Half Management Resources, 65 percent of respondents said that communicating clearly and frequently is the most important action to take when going through organizational change (Wolper 2016). People should never feel as if they don't know what's going on. Your content always needs to include what's happening and why.

Two other notes about content: Do your audience analysis and remember connectors. I once worked for someone who thought having secret Santas would be fun for employee morale. Each person drew a co-worker's name from a hat, and then once a week, for four weeks, we had to buy something and sneak it into their office or mailbox. Fun? For many, definitely not. To most of the staff, this just seemed like another assigned task. Secret Santa may work better for your staff than it did for ours, but we would have preferred to do something else. For example, someone in our area had a great idea: A latte machine on a cart that could come to any office. An alternative to the break room coffee pot? That would have improved morale.

Content is also about what to exclude. If you ever tell your staff that "we want to leverage synchronicity to. . . . " you have probably lost them at "leverage." Don't use jargon; cut to the chase. Tell your employees what you want them to do (or not do). You should also avoid content that creates negativity. I once watched a restaurant manager yelling at the cooks: "You people are killing me! How can you be this bad? We have customers waiting and you can't get food out! What's going on? You're killing me." Do you think that made them want to cook food faster? Was it motivational? I don't think so. Managers can create negativity in more subtle ways, too: "Someone has to go to the training." Has to go? You just said, in effect, "This training has no value, and no one would ever think of going unless it was mandated." Consider the negative implications of what you're saying: You have sabotaged the training by sending a disgruntled trainee, and you have sabotaged your relationship with the employee who is forced to attend.

Look back at the list of all the comments you make in a day. How many would be scored as positive in your employees' eyes? How many as negative? According to an article about praise-to-criticism ratio in the *Harvard Business Review*, research shows that while managers cannot avoid constructive criticism, high-performing teams had 5.6 positive comments for every negative comment, whereas low-performing teams had 0.36 positive comments for every negative one (Zenger and Folkman 2013). What is your ratio?

Visual Aids

Managers may use visual aids for meetings just as trainers do for training sessions. Reread step 5 to making effective aids. But managers should think about other visual aids. Walk into the break room at your workplace. How does it look? Walk into the bathroom and look around. Is it nice?

What does this have to do with visual aids? Managers sometimes miss the idea that the entire workplace is a visual aid. Here's what I mean: A trainer wants to give trainees the best possible help to understand the material. He wants his audience to know that this information matters and that he spent time making the presentation look good. Similarly, a manager should want to give employees the best possible environment so that they can produce results. She wants her audience to know that working conditions matter and that she spent time making the workplace look good. An ugly work environment is depressing and demoralizing—tattered posters and bare walls in desperate need of repainting scream, "You are not valued."

A messy work environment says attention to detail is not valued here. A cluttered environment says you are not in control. Your customers and clients will notice and leave with a bad impression. Your workers notice, too. This does not mean you should plaster the walls with inspirational art. Employees have seen the Teamwork, Attitude, and Above & Beyond posters. However, it does mean you constantly monitor what is on the wall: Is that outdated calendar still hanging in your office? Is that memo announcing an event last month still taped to the refrigerator? Look around with new eyes. What does your workplace say about you?

Performing a Talk

Everyone in your organization will expect you to be poised and audible, and to make eye contact appropriately. They will also notice if you have engaging gestures and use speed well to emphasize points. But managers will be more successful if they master the most difficult piece of performance: Life.

Life

It goes without saying that you need to speak with feeling. Look up and down your organization. How many of your senior leaders are impressive speakers? Running a staff meeting for 20 people requires good verbal skills. Moving up to district manager requires competence in the field, but presentation skills are also an important factor. What about the regional director? My guess is that presentation skills are more important than numbers. Do you need someone to talk to all the store managers in the northwest region? You'll want to promote the person with over-the-top performance skills who is full of energy and feeling. My point is that speaking well is the key to advancement for managers. To impress the audience above you, work on giving your presentations life. Life is just as important for impressing the audience working for you. You are their role model. You set the tone. Let your staff know the importance of improving this aspect of speaking.

At Starbucks, onboarding is largely done by 25 hours of online training. New employees learn information about store positions, health and safety, culture and coffee, blending drinks, and more online. That is followed up by in-store training, where barista trainers (veteran baristas who have been given three and a half hours of video training) will watch new hires at the register and at the bar. What is missing? The number one thing store manager Jason wants in his employees: life. He knows that if he wants his baristas to be great communicators, he'll have to train them to better their social skills and verbal communication. He tells his employees that they are actors. (Sound familiar? Speaking is performing!) In his words, baristas "should stand out the instant the customer walks in the store." He wants his employees to convey confidence and energy, even at 5 a.m., when most people may not feel up to the task (that's where acting comes in). He asks them to add life to their voices as if this was the best day ever and this customer is the greatest ever.

As a final comment about life, never let your tone of voice betray you. Like you, I have had some terrible managers. Remember Jane? I talked about her in step 10. She could play to an audience of superiors well, but was awful with the other audience, her employees. She knew enough to say, "I would be happy to get your input on this," but she said it in a way that made it clear that she couldn't care less. Jane needed to monitor the life in her voice. Don't let your tone of voice betray your words.

Digital Considerations

Why do we hold staff meetings? Because there have always been staff meetings, right? Wednesday mornings at 8. Every other Tuesday afternoon. The first Monday of the month. Here's a radical suggestion: Replace in-person meetings with digital meetings.

Why are so many organizations slow to adopt the use of technological tools for knowledge sharing? According to an article in *TD* magazine (Ho 2016), only a third of organizations use such tools. Digital communication and collaboration tools exist for hosting virtual meetings. Use them. Your company may use Yammer and TelePresence or competitors of those to facilitate online discussions. If not, some other options include Voice Thread, Flipgrid, and Slack. Instead of calling everyone to a meeting and interrupting their work flow, open a conversation online. Post an audio message or video, and send the link to your employees. They will respond whenever it is convenient. You could post pictures of the break room and ask for comments about how to improve the environment. You could post a video of a customer interaction and ask employees to critique what they see. VoiceThread allows you to upload a PowerPoint presentation for employees to watch and respond to asynchronously. Another option is Amplement, which provides a platform for chatting (think Slack), conferring (think Skype), document sharing (think Google Docs), and more.

Share ideas with your staff using Periscope, which lets you broadcast live video. Rather than have the staff meet in the conference room, set up your smartphone, open Periscope, and broadcast to your employees. If they have a Periscope account, they will receive a notification and can attend the meeting virtually. There are other uses for this type of program, such as broadcasting a new procedure or streaming an important part of a training session.

Regardless of which tool you use or how you use them, the real benefit of these tools is that they give your entire staff a voice. In a typical meeting, only a few people are heard from. Others may be intimidated by those few or they may not have ideas at that moment. Providing a digital voice option gives other employees the chance to think, record, erase, re-record, and share.

One more insight from Margaret McGuckin. She tells the story of a Millennial in one of the company's offices who thought that tasks were beneath him, didn't think he needed to learn much, and was difficult to manage. When she asked him how he saw his role in the company, he said that he didn't plan to stay with the company because he wanted to be a consultant. Margaret asked, "In what area?" "Oh, I don't know," he replied. "Well what are you an expert in? What expertise can you offer to potential clients?" she queried. He said, "I'm not sure, but I think being a consultant would be cool."

I'm guessing that every generation has thought that a younger generation is too full of themselves, but this example really indicates a willingness to teach, to be an expert. If there is an area in which Millennials are likely to excel, it is using digital tools. Harness that. Give them the lead in moving from in-person to digital meetings. Task them with using sites such as Adobe Spark or Mysimpleshow to create instructional materials or small sales presentations. They will likely know of several other ways to create digital content. At some point, you will have a digital library of resources to share in your onboarding process, and your future consultants will have an outlet for their creativity and expertise.

15

11-Step Speaking in the Workplace

What if you aren't a manager, trainer, or instructional designer? You will still find the 11 steps to be very helpful. Every job involves verbal communication. People with communication skills who stand out are more successful than others. You notice the difference immediately. One morning while I was waiting in line to have my car serviced, I had the chance to watch the four service specialists checking in the customers who had appointments that day. At Jana's window, the customers were smiling; at the other three, they were simply completing tasks. The difference? The service specialists all said the same thing, but Jana added something special to the basic, "The estimate is $239.67. Please sign here. We'll call you." She performed better—her life, eye contact, and engaging facial gestures said, "I'm glad you're here." Whose customers will go back to work and talk up the dealership? Jana's.

When I got to work, I ran into our building engineer. John was hired because we needed a handyman who could fix all the little things that go wrong and keep everything running smoothly. We liked the way he did his business, but we loved his communication skills. He created a special message for each of us every day. John knew I loved baseball, so he greeted me with, "How about those Tigers? They doin' well?" He was a performer. Every one of us noticed how fun and engaging it was to talk to John. He contributed nothing but positive energy to the workplace atmosphere. We don't think of service specialists and building engineers as speaking professions. Even so, communication skills matter. A lot.

Sales

There are thousands of books that offer sales tips. It's overwhelming. Use the 11-step framework to help you find the right one for you. What do salespeople do? They create and deliver presentations. If a sale is lost, was it because the presentation was poorly created? Review steps 1 through 5 and redesign your talk using the ideas there. Why do some salespeople excel? They give special attention to one aspect of content: They use connectors. Does your competition know more about the business and the buyers than you do? If so, your chance of success goes down dramatically because you won't be able to connect. Find ways to connect the product directly and exactly to the specific needs of the customer. There is no generic sales pitch—if you don't know my issues, you cannot connect your product or service to my situation. Find ways to connect personally with the people who make the purchasing decisions. Remember the ketchup fiasco in step 1? In addition to avoiding such mistakes, find common ground. "I like you" influences "I like your product."

Was good material poorly presented? Look back at steps 6 through 11. Improve your weak areas. Give special attention to life. Where are you on the grid in Figure 15-1?

True, your competitor may have a better product. But you're concerned about whether an inferior product seemed superior because the communication skills of their sales staff were superior. The most important skill? Life. You don't deserve sales if you are in quadrant 1. You lose sales you should have if you are in quadrant 2. Sure, you want to be in quadrant 4, but a lot of sales are also made in quadrant 3.

Figure 15-1. How Building and Performing Affect Sales

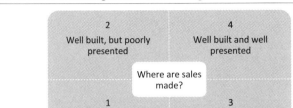

In all speaking genres, your performance skills are more influential than creating skills. Don't misunderstand: I am not trying to add to the world's number of slick salesmen who fast-talk their way into deals. I trust that you believe in what you are selling, and I have been clear that life doesn't mean faking something to trick your audience. Life means you don't just deliver your presentation; rather, you display vocal communication skills that are truly impressive.

Top salespeople are often referred to as "top performers" on company charts. That needs to have a double meaning: Yes, they out-performed others on company quotas, but they also out-performed with their superior communication skills. They usually have the same materials as the other salespeople, so the trick isn't in creating the talk. The trick is in making that material seem fantastic. Lively and engaging inflection connects on an emotional level. Never underestimate the affect of emotion on sales.

Interviews

Are you interviewing for a better position or with a different company? If so, you need to create a winning message. Focus on audience and content. Know the audience—manager or hiring committee—and design your answers for them. At some point in the interview, you want to be able to say, "I have been following your company for years and have great respect for the way your company [*insert detail about the company*]. You value [*insert detail*] and people have said great things about [*insert detail*]."

Add content that will show why you are the superior choice. Thea Kelley of Thea Kelley Career Services suggests adding content that persuades rather than informs. Running through a resume is boring—every interviewee says the same thing and tosses in the same jargon. Don't repeat, stand out. Think of two or three key differentiators, to use Kelley's term—skills or accomplishments that set you apart. Emphasize skills that are relevant, exceptional, and provable. Do they want communication skills? What is it about your communication skills that separates you from the rest? How can you prove it? Use stories to help sell your message: "I wrote the handbook for our field technicians. Calls from them to the support desk dropped 40 percent. One tech, Turk, sent me a thank you note saying I made his job so much easier."

These differentiators are perfect for closing your interview. "Thank you for your time" is polite but does not set you apart. Instead, say thank you first, and then come back to that best qualification: "Thanks for your time. I love what I heard today, and I think my [*insert best qualification or two*] will really contribute to this job." Don't forget to add connectors: "I noticed a picture of the little girl in the soccer uniform. Does she play for Lightning [the community soccer club]?" Show that you know your audience and bring yourself closer to them.

Be a winning performer. Focus on poise and life. Rehearse all possible answers so nothing surprises you and takes away your poise. When you hear, "Tell me about yourself," use Thea's advice to create a winning answer. How would you answer "Tell me about a time when. . ." or "Why did you leave your previous company?" Search online to find offbeat questions that might be asked. Be prepared.

Finally, add life. Are you passionate about your skills and about the job? Make sure that can be heard in your voice. You have a very limited time to impress those interviewing you. Competence and confidence are revealed by a voice that conveys feeling, emotion, and passion. If you sound flat, you won't ignite interest in yourself. If we hear how cool it was to have Turk send you a thank you note, we will be impressed.

Customer Contact

Are you in a consumer- or customer-facing role? Improved speaking will improve your success at work. Most of the time you'll have to create messages very quickly—someone walks into the office or up to the counter and you are on.

How quickly do you think on your feet? That is a way of asking, "How quickly can you create a response?" Review steps 1 to 5, focusing on audience and content. If you have been in the business a while, you can probably categorize your audience. This will often help you figure out how to deal with an individual, but remember that they are individuals. The "crotchety old woman" may surprise you by turning out to be a sweetheart. As for content, you have been trained about basic content: "Here's what to say when. . ." "Here's what to do if. . ." "Here's how to greet. . ." "Here's how to answer. . . ." You have also been coached in how to deal with difficult customers. So, when a difficult situation arises, the temptation to say, "Get out of my office, jerk," is overridden and you use defusing statements instead, right?

In your job, performing the message is the key. Focus on life and eye contact. I recently watched a woman at the United Airlines service counter dealing with a difficult customer. Bad weather at one of their hubs delayed many flights; although the skies were clear where we were, our flight to Denver was delayed due to a late inbound aircraft. This particular customer was irate because he was going to miss his connection at the Denver airport. I'm sure you have witnessed a similar scene: a screaming person who is mad at someone who had nothing to do with the problem and is in fact trying to help. Chris, the United employee, was amazing. The life in the customer's voice? Anger. The life in her voice? Kindness and empathy. She stayed calm and rebooked him, even as he heaped abuse on her. I wonder if later he thought, "I ought to apologize. I was way out of line." I don't know if he sent a letter to United to commend Chris for exceptional customer service, but I did. Focus on the life you add to your voice. It can be a real performance, acting in its truest sense. I've said repeatedly that the number one growth area for all speakers is life. The number one way to succeed at customer-facing jobs is to control the life in your voice.

Look at customers and clients directly and often. Failing to look at them costs you the chance to bond with them. Averting your eyes makes customers think they are not important, not worth your time. Trade places with your customer. Imagine that you are at the counter. Version A: The employee behind the counter never looks up, but says, "Just a minute." Version B: The employee behind the counter looks up, looks right at you, and says, "Just a minute." For which employee are you willing to wait? Being seen is being acknowledged; being acknowledged is the beginning of being connected.

Service Providers

Why should someone hire you for a landscape job? Why should someone contract with you to put in a new electrical panel? There are nail salons at every strip mall; why should someone choose yours? It is not usually about cost. It is about communication. If you present your idea well and if you are fun to talk to, you will get more business. Sure, word of mouth from a job well done is valuable, but more is needed. Remember Dave, the drywaller? He did good work, and he had strong oral communication skills. His special talent? Connecting. He could quickly build rapport with potential customers and, importantly, made his workers and his clients believe they were valued individuals. Develop your communication skills and, no matter what business you are in, success will follow.

16

11-Step Speaking for Social Situations

We talk. Often that talk is not particularly important: Idle chat passes the time, and casual conversations include amusing situations and discussions of current events. Most of us don't worry about that type of talk. A best friend calling to suggest meeting for lunch does not lead to worrying: "What am I going to say? What if I mess up? I'm not good at this!" So why do we have those thoughts for other speaking situations? What changes? Why are some talks scarier?

Is it audience size? You may be fine talking to one or two people, but the number of listeners at the wedding is daunting. Is it the importance of the talk? Retelling a story from your vacation is one thing, but proposing marriage is another. Is it the strangeness of the audience? You're good with people you know, but you fear the judgments of people you don't. Is it the uniqueness of the talk? You've never spoken at a funeral before. Is it all of those?

You are not alone. Almost everyone has a fear of speaking that kicks in at some point. As I stated, knowing how to create and perform effective talks diminishes that fear. It doesn't matter what the situation is; the 11 steps will help. You may believe that you already have all the information you need to succeed with social talks. That's great. But if you'd like a bit more help, read on for a brief discussion about some types of talks and the most significant concerns for the talk involved.

One to One

What if the audience is only one person? What if you know that person really well? No problem, right? Not in my experience. Think of personal talks that are common and yet high stakes: giving your 16-year-old son the car keys for the first time; dropping your daughter off at college; telling your spouse that you want a new job; talking to your mother about moving into assisted living; telling your daughter about a divorce; explaining to your three-year-old son that Grandpa has died; giving the lecture about the birds and the bees and the power of sexual attraction; and many more. These are not easy talks. Use the 11-step framework for each one, and pay special attention to audience and content.

Failure to understand your audience will lead to ineffective talks. We often don't do enough to imagine what is going on inside the head of the listener, so we fail to design a talk specifically for that individual. Let's look at some examples.

What does a three-year-old understand about death? How can you convey that Grandpa will never come visit again? A three-year-old brain cannot grasp the finality of death. (The Fred Rogers Company has great resources to help parents with this problem.) The point here is that all brains have blind spots—places where your words won't make sense.

What does a 16-year-old boy think about driving? He is thrilled. He thinks he's bulletproof and that he will never make bad decisions. Maybe you threaten, "I won't pay for insurance if. . ." or "I will take back the keys if. . ." or "If your grades go down. . ." It doesn't matter; none of that applies to him! You are worried about nothing. (You were there once yourself, remember?)

What does an aging mother think about assisted living? She is positive she is still competent; she values independence; she loves the house where all the kids grew up; she won't fall and break a hip. You are worried about nothing. (You might be there yourself one day.)

You may see a more realistic picture, but they can't because of their mindset. Never ignore the way your audience filters your message. Be aware that repeating the words a few times more loudly won't get past their filters. Figure out what part of your message will not be heard because the listener's mind is incapable of hearing it.

With that knowledge, you can shape your talk. Include questions such as:

- What is going on inside your head?
- What do you think the odds are that...?
- If you were in my position, what would you be thinking? Why?
- What do you think I am trying to accomplish?

The goal is get your audience to analyze themselves and you. You want the listener to understand that your message isn't a bunch of generalities and statistics. It's not from the authority to an underling. Your only chance of success is when the listener understands that you are sharing person-to-person concerns. Connect, then talk.

Parties

Parties are supposed to be fun. For many, however, they are quite the opposite. Meeting strangers, making small talk, avoiding a faux pas, being forced to act like an extrovert—these are stressors. Think before you go. Understand the audience. Who will be at the party? What do you know about them? That will help you come up with content. Some can come up with life-of-the-party repartee on the spot. Other people need help. Debra Fine, author of *The Fine Art of Small Talk,* was an engineer and realized that many in her profession were not social butterflies. Part of the problem? They couldn't think of what to say. Her book is full of content suggestions: questions to ask to start conversations, ways to respond that keep conversations going, phrases to avoid, and more. The truth is that you can create content for a party just as you create content for a speech. Don't put yourself on the spot. Prepare.

Toasts

Bachelor or bachelorette party, wedding, dinner party, family reunion, retirement celebration, farewell party—you may have attended many of these events. They all involve toasts. People always ask, "What should I say?" That is a content question.

Remember what I said in step 2: Why you? Why do people think you should be one of the people toasting? You must have some special relationship, so share a story about that. But keep it short—three minutes is a good time limit.

Match the mood of the occasion. At a farewell dinner, roasting the person leaving is probably inappropriate. Think of something sentimental instead. For the bachelor or bachelorette party, humor is important. To toast the hosts of the dinner party, a polite and formal acknowledgment is called for. Remember that you are not the focus here. Listeners should not be thinking about you and your speechmaking, but rather about the honoree. Shine a spotlight on him or her with some well-designed comments, take a sip from your glass, and sit down.

Speeches

Actions speak louder than words. You have heard that before, and you know it is true. What you do is always more important than what you say. When creating content for longer talks, it's best to describe actions. The person you are talking about comes alive when you give examples of what they did. A typical eulogy sounds a lot like:

> *My father had a good sense of humor even in tough situations. He also had a healthy disrespect for authority. He wasn't afraid to take chances. I admired that in him.*

Listeners get a sense of the father, don't they? Not bad. Now consider this:

> *My father spent two and a half years in the South Pacific during World War II. He was stationed on a remote island cut off from civilization for*

the most part, but not cut off from occasional Japanese bombing raids. Once in a while, a supply ship would arrive with Spam, censored letters from home, and news. One of my father's jobs was to take the news and turn it into the Jungle Journal, a little newspaper that was then given to the servicemen. Turns out the base commander was from Texas and always made a point of showing his Texas pride. My dad saw an opportunity to give the commander little jibes. If the news said, "Victory gardens are a huge success. Most states are exceeding their production quotas," the Jungle Journal would say, "Victory gardens are a huge success. Every state except Texas is exceeding production quotas." If the news said, "Nylon rationing is working. Women back home are cutting back to support the war effort," the Jungle Journal would say, "Nylon rationing is working except in Texas, where women are not cutting back to support the war effort." One day, the commanding officer was looking over his shoulder as he typed. "Victor, I think you ought to remove that line about Texas." Busted.

It takes one minute and 15 seconds to tell that story. Listeners get a chance to see Victor in action and, through that story, get a good idea of his sense of humor, his insubordinate streak, and his willingness to take risks. Of the two versions, which one is more memorable?

I talked about stories in step 2. They *must* be used in speeches for weddings, funerals, retirement dinners, bar and bat mitzvahs, sermons on layperson Sunday, graduations, and other occasions that call for more than just a toast. Choose a story that reveals an insight into the person being talked about. Choose a story that will get an emotional response. In the story about Victor, listeners will experience amusement. For other talks, you may want a story that triggers sadness or joy. Add details to make the story vivid. Notice the mention of Spam and censored letters in Victor's eulogy. They're not key to understanding the father, but they're useful for making the tale come alive. Think about incorporating our five senses: let us see, hear, feel, smell, and taste as appropriate to create a powerful image in our minds.

And of course, add some life. I once worked with a woman who was going to speak at her daughter's wedding. She was afraid that she might cry as she told a story about her little girl. Afraid? That would be perfect!

Listeners want to hear feeling. Genuine emotional arousal is ideal, not something to be afraid of. Never hide feeling, emotion, or passion. You may not have such dramatic life in your talk, but there should be some. In the story about Victor, I'd give the commanding officer's line with a Texas accent and in a different, deeper voice than my natural voice. How would you say, "Busted"? The same way you would if speaking the sentence, "She cut her foot on the busted bottle"? I hope not. I bet it would take longer to get the word out, for one thing: "BUSSSS-tid!" Look for opportunities to add inflection.

Remember to visit www.ownanyoccasion.com, the *Own Any Occasion* website, where you'll find ideas and exemplary talks. In fact, feel free to contribute successful talks you have given or witnessed! Crowdsourcing is a great way to develop resources. Of course, you don't need to add to the site. You just need to know that if you master VOCAL preparation and PVLEGS performance, you will own any occasion. Enjoy!

Acknowledgments

This book is the result of Tim Ito's idea. Tim is a senior director at ATD. He and I became acquainted when he was working for ASCD, a publisher of some of my other books and materials. He understood the value that improved oral communication would have for those in ATD's sphere of influence and asked if I would be willing to share my ideas for improving speaking with this audience. Thanks, Tim, for the opportunity and for valuing my work.

While we are on the subject of ATD, Christian Green was the editorial manager there. He took the words I wrote and made them better. He passed the torch to Melissa Jones, who polished up my manuscript and made brilliant suggestions for revisions. It is always great fun for me to see how editors can rephrase things, point out places that need clarification, and suggest additions that improve a manuscript. Thanks, Christian and Melissa, for excellent tweaks.

To make the book specifically relevant for the audience Tim had in mind, I attended ATD's International Conference & Exposition. There, I ran into Jean Marrapodi of Applestar Productions. I don't usually go up to strangers and interview them, but I needed a little education about trainers and training, so I sat down next to Jean and interrupted her lunch. I got lucky. Jean is clearly a master trainer herself and an expert about training in general. She could not have been more gracious or more helpful. Thanks, Jean, for your wisdom and openness.

Dan Hendricks has been training and teaching for quite a while. Now at a Fortune 500 company, he was quick to recognize that improved speaking skills would benefit the trainers he supervises. Dan brought my frameworks for creating and performing talks to his workplace and gave me valuable feedback. Thanks, Dan, for seeing the importance of improving your staff's communication skills and for verifying that all speakers can improve.

Barb Rarden, senior organization development consultant with Teradata, and Margaret McGuckin, now a co-founder of i3 Ignite, have lived on the front lines of training and management. They have expertise and experience from years of success developing talent. Their thinking was instrumental in helping me tailor the speaking skills framework for the workplace. Thanks, Barb and Margaret, for your insights.

Jason Walker is the manager of a Starbucks location in Oregon. He is passionate about helping his associates succeed and recognizes that excellent communication skills play a part in their success. Jason has an uncommon amount of common-sense, which showed up as he shared ideas with me. Thanks, Jason, for your practical input.

My wife, Anne, is mentioned a few times in the book. She contributed ideas about how to open a talk, about how to gesture, and more. Mostly, though, she supported the entire process of writing this book. Anne has always given me excellent moral support when I embark on new projects. She also provides a different kind of support: delaying dinner when I am in writing mode, sneaking into the office to refresh coffee, and tolerating lights coming on in the middle of the night so I can write down an idea. Small things, perhaps, but meaningful. Thanks as always, Anne, for being wonderful.

References

Achor, S. 2011. "The Happy Secret to Better Work." TedxBloomington, May. www.ted.com/talks/shawn_achor_the_happy_secret_to_better_work

Branson, R. 2014. "Look After Your Staff." Virgin.com, March 27. www.virgin .com/richard-branson/look-after-your-staff.

Carlin, G. 1997. *Brain Droppings.* New York: Hyperion.

Carr, N. 2011. *The Shallows: What the Internet Is Doing to Our Brains.* New York: W.W. Norton.

Cho, M. 2016. "Why Being Polite Is Killing Your Company." *Inc.,* November 2. www.inc.com/mikael-cho/why-being-polite-is-killing-your-company.html.

Cole, M. 2016. "Employee Knowledge Sharing Helps Nurture a Culture of Learning." *TD,* May. www.td.org/Publications/Magazines/TD/TD-Archive/2016 /05/Employee-Knowledge-Sharing-Helps-Nurture-a-Culture-of-Learning.

Delpit, L. 1995. *Other People's Children.* New York: The New Press.

Fry, R. 2015. "Millennials Surpass Gen Xers as the Largest Generation in U.S. Labor Force." Pew Research Center, May 11. www.pewresearch.org/fact-tank /2015/05/11/millennials-surpass-gen-xers-as-the-largest-generation-in-u-s-labor-force.

Harrell, T.W., and B. Alpert. 1986. "Attributes of Successful MBAs: A Twenty-Year Longitudinal Study." Working Paper No. 898. Stanford Graduate School of Business. www.gsb.stanford.edu/faculty-research/working-papers /attributes-successful-mbas-twenty-year-longitudinal-study.

Ho, M. 2016. "Investment in Learning Increases for Fourth Straight Year." *TD* Magazine, November. www.td.org/Publications/Magazines/TD/TD-Archive /2016/11/Investment-in-Learning-Increases-for-Fourth-Straight-Year.

Kohn, A. 2014. "Brain Science: The Forgetting Curve—The Dirty Secret of Corporate Training." *Learning Solutions Magazine,* March 13. www.learningsolutionsmag. com/articles/1379/brain-science-the-forgetting-curvethe-dirty-secret-of -corporate-training.

Mainwaring, S. 2015. "Starbucks Finds Itself in Hot Water for Talking About Race." *Forbes,* March 23. www.forbes.com/sites/simonmainwaring/2015/03/23/starbucks-finds-itself-in-hot-water-for-talking-about-race/#6e985db21b59.

Mayer, R. 2009. *Multimedia Learning,* 2nd edition. New York: Cambridge University Press.

Mills, H.R. 1977. *Techniques of Technical Training,* 3rd edition. London: Macmillan.

Raymundo, O. 2014. "Richard Branson: Companies Should Put Employees First." *Inc.,* October 28. www.inc.com/oscar-raymundo/richard-branson-companies-should-put-employees-first.html.

Teem. 2016. "You Can't Buy Workplace Happiness, But Tech Helps: Infographic." Based on EventBoard's Employee Happiness Survey. http://info.teem.com/workplace-happiness-infographic.

Torlakson, T. 2016. "Launching the 2014 ELA/ELD Framework." Santa Clara County Office of Education; California Department of Education presentation. April 25. www.mydigitalchalkboard.org/cognoti/content/file/resources/documents/c9/c9481f14/c9481f143987707fabddd27a18fac6b5dbffca6a/SantaClaraContent Knowledge612PPT_MDC.pdf.

University of Kent. n.d. "Top 10 Employability Skills." www.kent.ac.uk/careers/sk/top-ten-skills.htm.

Williams, T. 2016. "Employers Say Verbal Communication Is the Most Important Skill for Job Candidates, Reveals New Report." Good Call, May 4. www.goodcall.com/news/employers-say-verbal-communication-important-skill-job-candidates-reveals-new-report-06504.

Wolper, J. 2016. "Making Change Management Successful." *TD,* May. www.td.org/Publications/Magazines/TD/TD-Archive/2016/05/Intelligence-Making-Change-Management-Successful.

Zenger, J., and J. Folkman. 2013. "The Ideal Praise-to-Criticism Ratio." *Harvard Business Review,* March 15. https://hbr.org/2013/03/the-ideal-praise-to-criticism.

Zolfagharifard, E. 2014. "First Impressions Really Do Count: Employers Make Decisions About Job Applicants in Under Seven Minutes." DailyMail.com, June 18. www.dailymail.co.uk/sciencetech/article-2661474/First-impressions-really-Do-count-Employers-make-decisions-job-applicants-seven-minutes.

About the Author

Erik Palmer brings his unique experiences to his work as a consultant, speaker, and author, showing people in all walks of life how to become confident, competent communicators.

In his first career, Erik managed a commodity trading office for a major Chicago brokerage firm and was their national sales leader. He was also a floor trader on a Chicago commodity exchange. After his sons were born, Erik began teaching. During his 20 years in the classroom, he was named teacher of the year in one of the nation's most prestigious school districts.

A frequent presenter at conferences, Erik has given keynotes and led training sessions for many organizations and companies. His work has taken him across the United States and around the world. He is the author of *Well Spoken* (Stenhouse Publishers, 2011), *Digitally Speaking* (Stenhouse Publishers, 2012), *Teaching the Core Skills of Listening & Speaking* (ASCD, 2013), *Researching in a Digital World* (ASCD, 2014), *Good Thinking* (Stenhouse Publishers, 2016), and *Own Any Occasion* (ATD, 2017).

Erik grew up in Detroit. His educational background includes Southern Methodist University, Oberlin College, the University of Denver College of Law, and the University of Colorado. He lives in Aurora, Colorado, with his wife, Anne, and spends a lot of time traveling to work, on cycling vacations, and visiting grandchildren.

Index